Park City Hiking Guide

2nd Edition

By Beverly Hurwitz MD

Surrogate Press®

ALSO BY BEVERLY HURWITZ
Park City Walking Guide 2nd Edition
Nobody Else's Business - A Novel
Is the Cat Lady Crazy?

Published in the United States by
Surrogate Press®
an imprint of Faceted Press®
Surrogate Press, LLC
Park City, Utah
SurrogatePress.com

ISBN: 978-1-947459-52-6

Library of Congress Control Number: 2020924379

Book cover design by: Beverly Hurwitz

Interior design by: Katie Mullaly, Surrogate Press®

Photography by the author except where noted otherwise.

Table of Contents

Pandemically Speaking

At the time this book was being updated in the life-changing year of 2020, the future was uncertain and there were no indicators that the resort town of Park City would soon get back to normal. Still, this book was written with the hopes that people will ultimately be able to safely resume socialization and travel. In the meantime, Park City hikes have been impacted by COVID-19 in two major ways.

On the positive side, many more people have taken up hiking for exercise and recreation. This became apparent as soon as the ski resorts abruptly closed on March 15, 2020, and indoor exercise facilities lost their appeal. Park City's trails became busier than normal, and this book can help hikers to find lesser known routes.

Unfortunately, the pandemic has also resulted in a significant reduction of Park City's **free public bus service** that enables hikers to get to preferred terrain. A blue bag over a bus stop sign indicates the stop isn't currently served. Seek current information about Park City's bus service at *go.parkcity.org/ InfoPoint/ or parkcity.org/departments/transit-bus*.

Driving to trailheads can be problematic because **parking is limited,** and development keeps devouring what little is left. Paid parking will probably become the norm as demand grows and open land shrinks. Also, you never want to park in an unauthorized place, not even for a few minutes. The **risk of getting towed is high** and **so is the cost**.

You could walk to your destination. Having a friend or a driver service drop you off is another option. Hopefully, bus service will be restored and the bus instructions for these walks will be viable if not the most convenient way to get there, once the pandemic is behind us.

Historically, Park City was an early **hotspot** for COVID-19, probably because it hosts visitors from around the world. There's speculation that the corona virus had already arrived in Park City in January 2020, when Sundance Film Festival attendees with fevers were testing negative for influenza. COVID in the USA hadn't yet been recognized, and those who suffered the symptoms called their illness the "Festival Flu." My husband and I contracted COVID-19 in early March. My husband spent three weeks on a ventilator and miraculously survived. Eight months later, neither of has completely recovered from this vicious virus.

A mask mandate in Summit County reduced the incidence of COVID over the summer, but as I am writing this in late 2020, the incidence of infection is rapidly rising. Whether you live here or are visiting, please follow guidelines for **mask wearing, hand washing**, and **social distancing**. The life you save may be your own or someone dear to you.

Hopefully, the next time I update this book, information regarding the pandemic will not need to be included.

Introduction

It was the 1950s. My family lived in a suburban development that had once been a Long Island potato field. There were no trees except for the few that the conscientious developer planted amongst the tiny tract houses that sprang up after WWII along newly paved highways.

I was maybe seven when I got scolded for walking in a strip of trees between my street and a nearby parkway. "Little girls don't walk in the woods," I was told, even though those "woods" were barely three trees deep. Mom's gone now, so I can confess that I went back to those woods repeatedly to climb the trees, jump in the leaves, and watch the birds and other critters that lived there. It wasn't because I was a rebellious child; to the contrary, I was quite obedient. It was because I was then, and still am compelled to walk amidst trees. The first home I purchased as a young teacher was in New York's Catskill Forest Preserve, where I hiked amidst mighty oaks. Other residences I've lived in were always chosen for their proximity to hiking and skiing.

In 1990, a career opportunity enabled me to move to Park City. As soon as I arrived, I scouted out trails near my home in the Snyderville Basin where I could walk my dogs. Blissfully content with the paths I discovered in the old Park West ski area, and what would ultimately become Round Valley, I didn't initially go looking for alternative routes.

Then, some of "my" trails at Park West succumbed to development, and I needed to find new ones. I discovered a book, *Park City Trails*, but Park City had grown so rapidly since its 1984 publication, that almost none of the landmarks for the included trails were still identifiable. I knew there were trails through the trees around the resorts, but I didn't know how to access or navigate them, and I wound up bushwhacking when I tried. I worked nights and weekends in urgent care clinics then, so synching with other hikers wasn't convenient.

Meanwhile, in the mid 1980s, trail enthusiasts Charlie Sturgis and friends started sawing their way through Park City woods, when maybe only 14 miles (22 km) of trails were available. Their efforts, in conjunction with the grant writing and community organizing skills of trail devotee, Carol Potter, evolved into the **Mountain Trails Foundation**. This nonprofit, along with the help of many volunteers and community financial support, has managed to develop nearly **450 miles (724 km) of maintained trails** in and around Park City during the past three decades, with more to come. Partnered with a free public bus system that accesses most of these trails, Park City has become one of the most hiker friendly places in the world.

As a beneficiary of this expanding trail system over the decades, I came to take it for granted. Only when I set out to write this book did I come to realize how extraordinary Park City's trail system is, with seemingly more miles of trails than almost any city in the continental United States.

While some cities do boast of long trails that take you far away, Park City's hundreds of miles of trails are almost all in one place. As the crow flies, none of the hikes in this guidebook takes you more than 10 miles (16 km) from Old Town, or the greater Park City area's more than 170 restaurants, or state-of-the-art health care services. You can pretty much hike all day here and never quite leave town.

Unfortunately, there's a hitch to having so many trails in such a compact space; Park City's trail system is inordinately complex and tough to navigate. A map* of all of these miles of trails looks like a bowl of spaghetti, and old trail intersections aren't always shown because that would just crowd the map some more. Trying to learn routes on satellite images like those of Google Earth is frustrating because tree canopies make trails invisible. Although trail signage is  improving, many local trails remain unmarked. There's also the seasonal possibility that animals will create a new trail if nature provides a new food source.

Learning this trail system was a challenge, but once I did, I found it difficult to explain my routes to others. It was after a few "where do we go now?" phone calls from lost cousins that I realized that even experienced hikers need more than a map* to be able to navigate this incredible trail system, so I wrote *Park City Hiking Guide* to help other hikers find their way, with explicit directions and maps for 45 routes.

Many of these hikes are best accessed by Park City's free bus system, but directions for where to park are included. Many of these routes are accessible only after the snow melts, but depending on conditions, some trails are groomed in winter to facilitate hiking, snowshoeing, and other non-motorized activities.

This guidebook also provides information about health and safety issues related to hiking, high altitude exposure, sun protection, footwear, hiking gear, and hiking companions. All hikers are strongly encouraged to read the chapter on responsible hiking for personal safety and trail preservation, and become thoroughly familiar with wildlife encounter guidelines on page 19. Visiting hikers from sea level or low elevations, who have never previously hiked at high altitude, are encouraged to read the altitude chapter.

It's my hope that this book will help to make Park City's trails more accessible to hikers, who will in turn be more appreciative and respectful of this fantastic trail system and the life along its corridors.

Here's to safe, happy hiking, and, in the words of beloved Dr. Seuss:

You're off to great places.
Today is your day.
Your mountain is waiting.
So get on your way.

* I highly recommended that you purchase the **annual** trail map produced by the Mountain Trails Foundation as a supplement to this book. It will be your most up-to-date reference for new trails and trail changes. Sold in sporting goods stores around town, map sales help support the trails.

Why Hike? Why Not Hike?

For the purposes of this book, **hiking** means **walking on maintained trails in natural settings**. Access to **great trails** is in itself, a good reason to hike for exercise. Next time you think of heading for the gym on a nice day, go take a hike instead. A well-maintained trail system like Park City's allows exercisers to enjoy **different scenery** daily. Hiking can convert **exercise** from a repetitive chore to natural activity in a beautiful setting. Outdoor air can be a refreshing alternative to the atmosphere of perspiration and sanitizers found in indoor exercise facilities.

Hiking has numerous **physical health benefits**. It improves weight control, builds stamina, muscle strength and tone, improves respiratory and cardiovascular fitness, and supports bone density, immunity, and longevity. Regular hiking can reduce high blood pressure and cholesterol, mitigate diabetes and insomnia, and improve intestinal function. Blood levels of stress hormones are lower in people who spend time outdoors in natural environments than in those who are rarely in green spaces. Hiking can ease pain by releasing endorphins, the body's natural painkillers.

Hiking also boosts **psychological health**. Just the sounds of nature like a bird singing or a babbling brook have calming effects on the nervous system. This is also true for the scent of rich earth after a spring rain. Many people use recordings of nature sounds, or atomizers of nature's scents, to induce relaxation. Hospitalized patients who have a view of natural scenery show faster recovery times than patients whose windows face buildings.

Numerous scientific studies demonstrate that natural environments decrease negative emotions and boost a sense of well-being. Hiking can benefit persons suffering from depression, anxiety, substance abuse, and other common human afflictions. Hiking can nurture improvement in one's attention span and enhance creativity. Seniors who hike maintain better cognitive abilities like memory, than do people who do not walk for exercise. Children whose school programs include outdoor activities in nature, show improved skills in problem solving, critical thinking, leadership and teamwork. They also score higher on standardized tests.

Hiking can provide **private time** or strengthen **social bonds** with family and friends. Hiking presents opportunities to meet new people or spend time with your parents, children or dogs.

Hiking can be **easy.** There are trail options for most abilities. Though your hiking experience can be enhanced with special clothes and equipment, they aren't necessary. Hiking mostly requires motivation and some knowledge to keep you safe and optimize the experience. Hiking in Park City is especially easy. Most residents and visitors can find a trail within walking distance of their front door or hotel lobby.

Hiking provides exercise, transportation, recreation, and education. Many hikers find being out in nature spiritually enriching. One can hike for relaxation or challenge. Hiking can cultivate efficiency and self-sufficiency. Hiking allows you to live in the moment and have a sense of accomplishment. All of these benefits are available at NO COST.

So, why not hike? Unfortunately, hiking mountainous terrain at Park City's altitude isn't for everyone. Most of these hikes are at elevations of 7,000-10,000 feet (2,000-3,000 m).

Lowlanders with cardiovascular or respiratory disease may need to limit their hiking to more moderate elevations. Persons who do not feel fit enough to hike at lower altitudes should not attempt to hike in the mountains. Hiking in Park City requires a moderate level of **fitness, altitude tolerance,** and **greater stamina** than is needed to hike less demanding terrain.

Park City **trail surfaces are highly variable**. Although these trails are carefully maintained, streams rage, rocks roll, mud happens, and ignorant trail users leave footprints and ruts. A single hike might traverse smooth dirt, soft sand, hard clay, gravel, muddy gullies, weeds, roots, rocks, stone or wood bridges or steps, and sometimes, fallen trees.

Persons with limitations of **mobility, balance, agility,** or **vision**, or who are uncomfortable on terrain that requires **attentive footwork,** should limit walking to more reliable surfaces. In my previous book, *A Walker's Guide To Park City*, 30 routes are mapped out on mostly paved surfaces in and around town, local neighborhoods, and community parks. Routes for strollers and wheelchairs are also identified. If Park City hiking is not an option, many of the benefits of being outdoors can be achieved on the routes mapped out for walking.

PARK CITY
WALKING GUIDE
2nd Edition

Beverly Hurwitz MD

A Brief History of Hiking

Hiking wasn't always a recreational pursuit. Before canoes, horses and modern transportation, "hiking" was primarily a means of finding one's next meal. Hiking started to become a form of recreation in the 1800s, when people were moving away from rural life to work in factories. Industrialization and urbanization made humans long for their lost connection with nature.

With the development of public cemeteries in the1800s, urban dwellers started to stroll in these green spaces. As cities became larger and denser, people started to demand places to **"nature walk."** It was 1853 when the clamor of New Yorkers for paths amidst trees became so fervent, that plans for Manhattan's Central Park were born.

The 1854 publication of the book *Walden, Or, Life in the Woods*, by American author and activist, Henry David Thoreau, contributed to human romanticism for being able to spend time in a natural environment. The growing hunger for green space prompted communities all over the country to start building trails and parks. Hiking clubs formed and people from many walks of life voluntarily worked together to create and maintain trails between communities. Trails like the Appalachian Trail, running 2,200 miles (3,500 km) through the eastern United States, was conceived of in 1921 by a Vermont hiking club, and completed in 1937 by volunteers from more than 30 hiking clubs.

By the middle of the twentieth century, millions of Americans were using and, unfortunately, overusing trails, and developers were trying to commercialize them. This lead Congress and the administration of President Lyndon B. Johnson to create the **National Trail System Act of 1968**, which not only set regulations to protect existing trails, but provided funding to build more. As a result of this legislation, the United States now has a National Trail System of more than 50,000 miles (80,000 km) of noncommercial scenic, historic and recreation trails.

Unfortunately, there was a downside to this legislation. Federal government involvement led to a decline in volunteerism. News about trail construction with help from the NPS (National Park Service) and the BLM (Bureau of Land Management) made people interested in hiking, and in the 1970s, tens of thousands of people took up the sport. However, instead of devoting themselves to building and maintaining trails, most people invested in hiking gear at newly arising outdoor stores and crowded the trails some more.

Crowded trails prompted trail lovers and visionary municipalities to embrace the idea of local trail development. In Manhattan, citizens devoted themselves to converting an abandoned overhead rail line into a public park, and then they gave it to the city. In Park City, citizens and elected officials started to acquire rights of way and construct trails wherever they could.

When Congress passed the **1983 Rails-To-Trails Law,** thousands of miles (km) of long corridors of abandoned railroad tracks became available for trail development. Unfortunately, property rights lawsuits have delayed trail development in some places for decades, but in places like Park City, the rails-to-trails brainchild came to fruition. The tracks of the Union Pacific Railroad, which connected Park City with the Transcontinental Railroad up until the 1980s, have been replaced with 26 miles (42 km) of recreational trail.

Meanwhile, just in the past decade, trail construction has been revolutionized and Park City's trail system is a prime example of hiking's future. The loggers and miners who came to Park City's forests in the latter nineteenth century constructed trails and roads using axes, shovels, and horses to haul away rocks, earth and trees. In recent decades, volunteers with power tools and all-terrain vehicles (ATVs) more efficiently cleared paths through the forests. Now there's specialized heavy equipment such as the mini excavator and mini skid steer that have reduced the time it takes to construct a trail from an entire season to a few weeks. The skid steer, pictured here, is a tractor on cat tracks with a front blade that pushes away earth, rocks and vegetation. The excavator can move giant boulders, though trail builders sometimes design trails around boulders to show off the geology of the terrain. There's also a science to

designing trails. They're built to meander and undulate so that low spots act as drains. A slight downhill slope to the sides of the trail also facilitates drainage. Excavated dirt is deposited downhill so as not to wash back onto the trail. An experienced trail designer takes many things into account besides views.

With continued support from the community and trail users, Park City's expert trail builders hope to build more trails and provide more opportunities for people of most ability levels to enjoy Park City's deep mountain forests, fields of flowers, and spectacular scenery.

Perhaps humanity's connection with nature is coming full circle. The baby boomers, echo boomers, and generation Xers embraced the suburban culture of the automobile. The millennial generation seems less enamored with cars, and more inclined to live in walkable communities where hiking may again become, how people find their next meal.

Responsible Hiking

Hikers should dedicate themselves to leaving trails beautiful for all the trail users to come. **Trail preservation** is every hiker's responsibility and involves following a few simple rules:

1. **Stay on trails.** Shortcuts between trails cause **erosion.** Except for some municipal holdings, all of the land around Park City is privately owned, and it's only the generosity of landowners that allows public access. Wandering off trails onto private land could provoke landowners to restrict access to trails that run through their properties.

2. **Stay off of closed trails.** There could be a hazard or a race, and trails need maintenance. Closure may be designated by a sign, rope, log or rocks across the trail entrance. If your first-choice trail is closed, you have many other options.

3. **Stay off of wet** or **muddy trails.** Footprints can ruin a trail for an entire season and lead to erosion. If a trail surface **sticks to your heels, the trail is too wet to hike.** Trail conditions and closures in the Snyderville Basin can be found at the website: basinrecreation.org.

   The **Mountain Trails Foundation**, which created and maintains many local trails, provides daily reports on trail conditions on their website at *map.mountaintrails.org,* and on a smart phone app for subscribers.

   Please **check trail conditions before heading out for a hike** if there's been recent rain or snow, or you're unfamiliar with the trails or weather. If you encounter puddles or mud on an otherwise dry trail, it's kinder to the trail to walk through the muck than to widen the trail by walking around it. Should you be unfortunate enough to visit Park City during a wet week with intentions to hike, know that there are many alternative walks in Park City that won't damage trails. Interesting, scenic walking routes on paved surfaces are mapped and described in my previous book, *Park City Walking Guide.* Please consider that trail preservation should be a higher priority than your vacation plans.

4. **Leave trail amenities undisturbed.** It's always sad to see a bouquet of wilted wildflowers thrown to the ground at the end of someone's hike. Even plunged into a water bottle, most wildflowers are too fragile to survive once picked. Pretty flowers, rocks or interesting artifacts should be

left in place for the next appreciative eye. Unless you're lost and starving, berries should be reserved for the wildlife that depend on them.

5. **Leave no trace. If you packed it in, pack it out**. Even organic matter like orange or banana peels should go back in your lunch sack and back off the trail. They are more likely to become petrified litter than to decompose. **Used toilet paper must also be packed out,** preferably in a sealable baggy. On some of the hikes

Subalpine fir shows resin blisters on its bark and doesn't drop its pinecones. It's one of the three giant conifers along Park City trails. Douglas fir and Engelmann spruce drop their cones.
PHOTO by Wikimedia Commons

herein, there are few private places, and those spots are likely to provide bladder relief to many trail users. Imagine the scene if everyone left toilet paper. Leaves can substitute for toilet paper. Maple leaves work, and the soft, flexible needles of subalpine fir can function as a gentle brush. Avoid the stiff, sharp needles of spruces. Also avoid any plant that looks like poison ivy, as illustrated here.

Dog poop should also be carted away; no matter how far from the trail Rover does his business. Some trails provide dog waste bags and receptacles, but dog walkers should always bring their own in case these are not available. While we're on the subject of **poop**, there are two **options for human hikers**, and they both require planning ahead. Option one is to poop into a plastic bag and carry it out with you. Option two is to carry a trowel in your pack to dig a "**cat hole**". Make sure you're at least 65 yards (60 m)

ILLUSTRATION of poison ivy by Wikimedia Commons

away from trails and 100 yards (91 m) away from streams, and dig a hole 6-8 inches (15-20 cm) deep. Deposit the fecal material in the hole and then cover it up and disguise it, like a cat. This especially applies to diarrhea.

Self-preservation is the other major hiker responsibility. The hikes in this book are not long or remote, but even short, easy hikes can lead to problems if a hiker is unprepared for the unexpected. **If you plan to walk around in wilderness, you need to understand the risks.** According to the Centers for Disease Control, *www.cdc.gov*, hiking was the third most common outdoor recreational activity associated with injuries, (after snowboarding and sledding). Common hiker injuries include fractures, sprains and traumatic brain injury. In America's national parks, thousands of hikers require the assistance of Search and Rescue (SAR) Teams every year. You can see the park-by-park statistics at *www.nps.gov.*

Hiking accidents often result from lack of knowledge or experience. A hiker needs to know what to do if s/he encounters a forest fire, fire ants, a hungry bobcat, or other problems that can't be prevented. Experience will help hikers to develop good judgment, but **it's up to each hiker to obtain essential knowledge.** Storms, excessive temperatures, falling trees, a rockslide, a raging stream, or bear sightings are examples of **environmental risks. Topographic risks** include things like steep terrain, loose rocks, or a mineshaft unearthed by spring runoff. **Respect trail closures for your own safety.** There are also **human risk factors** such as overestimating one's fitness, altitude intolerance, or meeting up with another trail user whose behavior makes you uneasy. Wandering off trails could result in getting lost, having to climb out of a ravine, or getting arrested for trespassing. This guidebook offers information about some of the problems hikers might encounter and suggests ways to help prevent or manage these problems. However, please understand that following the advice provided in this book **cannot guarantee your safety.**

Reasons Why Hikers Trip and Fall and What To Do About Them	
Overestimating one's ability or **underestimating the trail**	Hiking requires some fitness and agility, and in Park City, altitude tolerance and stamina. Adequate vision and attentive footwork are also needed to navigate variable terrain. Persons unaccustomed to altitude or walking on inclines should test themselves on walks around town before hiking trails.
Fatigue	You're most vulnerable to tripping and falling if tired. Pace yourself for the length and steepness of the hike. Rest if tired and turn around and go downhill if rest doesn't help.
Steep terrain	Go slowly. Take small steps going uphill, leaning slightly forward at the ankles. When going downhill, a walking stick* can enhance stability. If it's very steep going down, **sidestep** (small sideways steps with feet perpendicular to the slope), or **traverse** (walk diagonally across the incline).
Slick terrain	Do not hike when trails are likely wet or icy. Turn around if it gets slippery. If you get stuck on slick terrain, walk like you're on a tightrope with tiny steps and arms out to the sides. Keep your head and torso upright and relaxed and knees a little bent. Sometimes, it's safest to go into a controlled slide on your feet or buttocks. Poles* may help.
Rocks and **roots** hidden under leaves	A walking stick* lets you feel the ground before you step. Proper footwear protects toes from getting stubbed.
Loose rocks or **gravel**	A walking stick* enhances stability. Go slowly. Plan each step. Be balanced on a stable platform before taking the next step.
Untied shoelace	Check laces at the start. Double knot your ties. Carry extras.
Poor visibility	Carry a bright flashlight if you're hiking around dawn or dusk.
Collisions with other trail users	Avoid camouflage clothing. Do not stop on trail curves, switchbacks or at intersections to answer the phone, etc. Wear reflective tape in front and back, and on the dog's collar at dawn or dusk. Cyclists with headlamps ride trails at night.
Distracted hiking	Texting while walking uneven terrain is risky. Listening to music or conversing can prevent hearing warnings from cyclists or a bugling elk. Step off the trail if preoccupied.
Inappropriate footwear	Poorly chosen or ill-fitting shoes can impede traction, balance, stability, agility, and stamina. See the chapter on footwear.

* A walking stick can be anything from a tree branch to trekking poles. Read about pole options in the gear chapter

Hikers can **learn how to reduce the risk of injury when a fall is inevitable.** Stuntmen and martial arts participants are some of the athletes who train to relax and roll away from falls. One can learn how to fall by practicing protective techniques on a sandy beach, on snow, or mats in a gym. Unless tumbling into water, wear a helmet to practice falling.

Protective Techniques For Falls	
Most people need practice to learn these techniques	
All falls	If you can't stop it, try to plan it. Relax. Drop softly. If possible, turn a forward or backward fall to sideways. Try to land on a fleshy body part like buttocks, thigh or shoulder. Tuck the chin to the chest to protect head, face, and neck. Flex elbows and knees. Don't try to break a fall with your hands. Avoid dreaded "foosh" wrist fractures (**f**ell **o**n **o**ut**s**tretched **h**ands).
Falling forward	Try to fall in a push-up position with forearms and hands flat on the ground and head turned to the side. Exhale.
Falling backwards	Squat with flexed knees, tucked chin, and arms flexed at sides to protect wrists. Be a ball. Try to land on your butt and then roll to one side.
Falling sideways	Squat with knees flexed. If falling right, try to land with the right arm and palm hitting the ground and the arm cushioning the head while holding the right hip with the left hand. Then try to roll from your side to your back. Reverse if falling left.

Unfortunately, not all mishaps can be prevented. **Wise hikers know basic first aid** and how to manage common problems like those listed (alphabetically) in the following table. Information about what first aid supplies to pack is provided in the gear chapter. Advice offered in this guidebook cannot substitute for having taken a first-aid course with hands on training, or using good judgment in a traumatic situation.

Hikers should also be up to date on **tetanus immunization**. Tetanus, a life-threatening infection, can result from even a minor scratch, but is easily prevented with vaccination.

Preventive Measures and First Aid for Common Injuries and Health Problems while Hiking	
All Injuries	Check airway, breathing and circulation and begin CPR if needed. Immediately call 911 if someone is unconscious, has difficulty breathing, severe chest pain or uncontrollable bleeding, or has maybe broken their neck, back or leg. When in doubt, call for help. Cell phone service is available in most Park City locations. Rescue teams are properly equipped to manage tough situations.
Altitude sickness	Preventable and treatable, but can be life threatening if unrecognized and improperly managed. Please read the chapter on altitude, health, and exercise.
Blisters	Apply moisturizer to clean feet before putting on socks. Don't go for a long hike in untested socks or shoes. Use a bandage or moleskin to cover hot spots before they blister. If you feel a pebble, sock seam, or other foot irritant, promptly fix the problem. If there's a blister, pop and drain it, leave the overlying dead skin in place, and clean and cover it with a bandage. Dead skin can be removed a few days later.
Broken bone	A suspected fracture of the head, neck, back, hip, leg, or foot requires rescue. A person with an arm or hand fracture might be able to hike to safety if adequately splinted. Immobilize the joints above and below the site of the fracture.
Cuts and scrapes	Immediately clean and bandage wounds to protect from infection. Cleaning is more important than applying an antiseptic. Large, deep, jagged or dirty cuts or punctures need medical follow-up. Lacerations that need stitches should be seen promptly.
Dehydration	An adult should consume at least 2 cups (0.5 L) of water per hour of hiking, more for hot temperatures or vigorous hikes. Kids need 1-2 cups (0.25-0.5 L) per hour. Drinking water before setting out on a hike, and taking sips along the way is the best way to stay ahead of dehydration. Avoid caffeinated beverages and alcohol, which increase water excretion. First aid is rehydration and rest. Dehydration associated with vomiting requires medical care. Read more about symptoms in the altitude chapter.
Fatigue	Had too much to drink last night? Not fully recovered from having a cold? Not really fit enough to keep up with buddies? Then don't go hiking! If periods of rest don't relieve a tired feeling, turn back or find the shortest way out and go slowly.
Frostbite Hypothermia	Avoid hiking in extreme cold and dress appropriately. Noses, fingers and toes are most at risk. Call for rescue if toes are frostbitten or body temperature is dropping. Do not attempt to walk on frostbitten feet and delay rewarming of a frostbitten part until in an environment where it can be kept warm. Keep the victim down and as warm as possible while waiting for rescue. Solar blankets are cheap and easily packed.

	Preventive Measures and **First Aid** for **Common Injuries** and **Health Problems** while **Hiking - CONTINUED**
Headache	This is often a symptom of dehydration or altitude sickness. If replenishing fluids and descending to lower altitude doesn't provide relief, and you're not normally a headache sufferer, medical consultation is advisable.
Head and/or **neck** *injury*	Even brief unconsciousness requires medical follow-up. Do not apply wound pressure if skull fracture is suspected. If sleepiness, odd behavior, vomiting or severe headache or neck pain develops, there could be bleeding or swelling inside the skull. Keep the person down and elevate the head, but do not flex or extend the neck if neck injury is suspected. Call for rescue.
Heat stroke	Avoiding exertion in extreme heat and adequate hydration are preventive. Cooling necklaces or bandanas and small packable fans are available. If someone's skin is red, hot and dry, and their level of consciousness seems impaired, you are dealing with a life-threatening emergency. Get the person to shade, lie them down, apply cool compresses if possible, and call for rescue.
Joint pain or sprain	Injuring the soft tissue around a joint can be just as debilitating as a fracture. Immediate first aid for an ankle sprain is to get off your feet and pull the affected foot up towards the knee, using your hand, belt or shirt, to relax the ligaments that just got stretched. A sprained ankle that's too painful to bear weight should not be walked on. Seek rescue. Hobbling on rough terrain is too risky.
Muscle cramps	Staying hydrated is preventive. Should one get a cramp while hiking, stop walking. Try to stretch and massage the spasmed muscle. Rest, and be sure the muscle is relaxed before resuming hiking. Medical follow-up is advisable for repeated episodes of cramping.
Poison ivy	Immediately remove contaminated clothing and wash the irritating oil off of your skin. Contaminated items like leather boots need to be aired out for a week. Oral antihistamines, and anti-itch creams can relieve symptoms. For a widespread or severe reaction, a physician may prescribe systemic steroids.
Shortness of breath	Stop hiking. Rest. This may be a symptom of altitude sickness if not a lack of fitness. If you can't get past the winded feeling, get to a lower altitude. If that doesn't help or you become lightheaded or have chest pain, call for help. Medical follow-up is recommended unless you're certain it was simply a matter of over-exertion.
Snake bite	Diamondback rattlesnakes may be encountered at lower altitudes. Get away from the snake; it could strike again. Get to a hospital immediately for **anti-venom**. Keep the bitten part as quiet as possible and below the level of the heart. Don't cut the wound, don't try to suck out the venom, and don't apply ice.
Sunburn	Please read the chapter on sun, sight and skin. If you burned anyway, cover up, get out of the sun, take a cool shower, apply an aloe moisturizer, and drink plenty of fluids. Ibuprofen or naprosyn may help pain. Don't rupture blisters. Monitor for infection.

Most insects pose no threat to humans and play important roles in the ecosystem. Park City's lack of **insect pests** (except for bark beetle infestation of forests) is one of its many blessings. However, animals moving along trails can carry fleas, ticks, etc. from one place to another.

Here's what hikers should know about biting bugs, just in case.

Protective Measures and **First Aid** for **Insect Bites**	
All bug bites	Hikers should carry a **first aid kit** containing oral antihistamine medication and antiseptic wipes. A topical anti-itch product to treat insect bites is a good addition. If available, ice helps itching. Monitor for signs of a systemic reaction and seek ER care if suspected.
Mosquitoes	Beware if there are puddles. Wear protective clothing and use repellent (discussed below) on exposed skin, especially in the evening if there's been recent rain. Hiking dogs need **heartworm** protection.
Spiders	Brown recluse and hobo spiders aren't too dangerous. The black widow spider bites if her eggs are threatened. She leaves two punctures followed by intense local pain. If pain spreads to torso and muscles, quickly get the victim to a hospital ER for **anti-venom.**
Bees	Bees can become agitated by fast moving people, especially on bikes. They may be attracted by scents like perfume, hair gel, etc., or clothes adorned with flowers or shiny jewelry. Don't allow children to hike with sweet juice or crumbs on their hands or faces. Stay calm if a bee buzzes you. If stung, remove bee stingers by flicking them. Administer oral antihistamine and topical cold or anti-itch product. Allergic persons should carry rescue kits and be taken to an ER if stung. The epinephrine (**Epipen**) in the emergency kit is very short acting.
Ticks	The ticks that carry Lyme Disease, rabbit fever, and Rocky Mountain Spotted Fever, and the American dog tick, are all found in Utah. Walk in the center of trails if there's tall vegetation on the sides. Insect repellent reduces the risk of bites. If dogs have walked through tall grasses, check for ticks before heading home. Do a thorough body inspection in the shower.
Fire Ants	If you or Rover disturbs a nest, you may get multiple painful bites that can burn for hours or cause a severe systemic reaction. Get away and immediately remove a sock or whatever they got into. It may be hard to pull or swat them off your skin when they clamp on. Try flicking them off. Take an oral antihistamine and apply ice if possible.

While applying **insect repellant** is rarely necessary for Park City hiking, I do use it if mosquitoes are present during an outbreak of West Nile Virus (WNV), a severe flu-like illness that can cause permanent brain damage or death. A compound called **DEET** is highly effective in preventing bites by mosquitoes and ticks. In use since the 1950s, most research suggests DEET is safe when used appropriately, even in pregnancy. The highest concentration of DEET necessary for protection is 30%, which can last for 4-6 hours. Apply DEET only to exposed skin and clothing. Spray shirts and pants on a hanger and let them dry before putting them on. Spray socks too. Infants under two months should be protected with mosquito netting instead of DEET.

Picaridin, a pepper derivative may be as effective and safer than DEET in a 20% concentration, but it's less well studied. Oil of lemon eucalyptus (OLE) is effective but is not recommended for use in children under three years.

A variety of products are available for flea and tick control for dogs, including oral medications, sprays, and even protective clothing. I've never caught a Park City flea or tick on my hiking shorthaired dachshunds, but they don't wander off the trails. Meandering, thick-coated dogs are more vulnerable. Check with the vet, especially regarding heartworm protection.

Much more likely than bug bites, **adverse weather** can turn a hike into a harrowing experience. If Mother Nature throws a curve ball, here's what you should know:

What To Do In Adverse Weather Conditions	
All conditions	With modern technology, there's no excuse for heading out for a hike in dangerous weather. Radar pictures that show current conditions are most useful. However, mountain weather is unpredictable. Unexpected microbursts of wind, rain, hail or snow can come out of nowhere, especially at higher elevations. Knowledge is the key to survival but does not guarantee safety.
Wind Storm or Tornado	Pay attention to weather reports, especially in Spring. Avoid hiking in the woods when high winds are expected. Some windstorms have knocked down hundreds of Park City trees with one or two giant gusts. Falling branches are another risk. Many aspens suffer from blight. Stay away from power lines and ski lifts. You may be safest lying face down in a clearing with your hands or pack protecting your head.
Fire	Lightning or careless humans can start a raging fire in seconds and in the drought-stricken west, fire spreads very rapidly. If you should see one, start moving downhill and into the wind. Though the path of a forest fire is highly unpredictable, they tend to spread up steep slopes toward passes and saddles, and through shrubbery. A rocky area, or place that has already burned may be the safest place to get to quickly. Call 911 as soon as you are out of imminent danger.

What To Do In Adverse Weather Conditions - CONTINUED	
Electrical storm	Electrical storms can pop up unexpectedly on hot afternoons. **Watch the skies.** Go downhill if a storm is brewing. **There's no place outdoors that is totally safe.** If the timing between a lightning flash and a clap of thunder is 30 seconds or less, seek immediate shelter. Stay there until 30 minutes after the last thunderclap. Lack of rain does not mean you are safe. "Dry lightning" is common. Get away from lone trees, open fields, rocky ridges, fences, power lines, ski lifts, or water. Leave your metal frame backpack, trekking poles, water bottles, iPods, etc., 100 feet (30 m) from where you take shelter. (Phone maybe okay?) Crouching down in a clump of small trees or brush is the best place to be, or in a low spot if in a meadow. Find the lowest place you can, crouch down in it, and if with a group, crouch at least 20 feet (6 km) away from others. If your skin starts to tingle or your hair stands up, a lightning strike is imminent. Crouch onto the balls of your feet with your feet close together, or drop to your knees and put your hands on your knees. Do not lie or sit. Do not put your hands down. You want minimal contact with the ground. If a person is struck by lightning, CPR may be necessary. Call for rescue.
Earthquake	Get down on your hands and knees before you get knocked down. Hold onto something if you can until the shaking stops. Cover your head. Before any aftershocks, try to get out into the open and away from rocks, trees, power lines, chairlifts, and anything that can fall.
Avalanche	Any backcountry activity in snowy mountains requires **formal avalanche training!** Find information about classes at *utahavalanchecenter.org/*

Park City's trails are for sharing. On some trails, hikers will frequently encounter **cyclists** and sometimes, big groups of cyclists. Electric bikes have also been given license and in winter, there may be cyclists on snow bikes. Bear in mind that cyclists built most of these trails but they are willing to share them with hikers. Most cyclists are courteous and friendly. However, some may

be inexperienced, unfamiliar with trail etiquette, or out of control and terrified. Even though hikers technically have the right of way, hikers should always be on the defensive when interfacing with cyclists.

The polite thing for hikers to do when encountering cyclists on single-track is to

step off the trail, if possible to the higher side of the trail. If cyclists don't tell you of stragglers, ask the last one who goes by if they *are* the last, before stepping back onto the trail. The polite thing for cyclists to do if coming from behind is to give hikers a loud warning as soon as possible. If hikers do not hear the warning, the cyclist should stop and make better effort to communicate. Advance warnings may not be possible when trail users meet each other head-on, coming around curves. Both hikers and cyclists should then stop and assess how many people need to be accommodated for safe passing.

Some trails are designated downhill biking only, meaning no uphill biking. Hiking these trails may be permissible if the hiker stays alert and cautious and yields the trail to bikers. Avoid these trails at busy times.

Expect to share winter trails with **snowshoers** and Nordic **skiers**. Skiers sometimes accrue unstoppable downhill speed, and like cyclists, their approach can be silent. Hikers may share some trails with equestrians. **Horses** spook easily, so verbal warnings are advised before coming close or passing. Take directions from riders.

Although cyclist encounters are most common, **wildlife** encounters are possible. One of the great joys of hiking is getting to watch a wild animal from a safe distance. If you hike here enough, you are likely to see mule deer, elk, moose, porcupines, marmots, tree squirrels and ground squirrels, rabbits, weasels, rodents, harmless snakes, and birds galore. If you hike at night with infrared lenses, you may see nocturnal hunters like bats, skunks, raccoons, beavers, bobcats, cougars, or coyotes. Bears also reside locally but are rarely seen. Some trailheads post warning signs like this coyote notice. Here are the basics to know:

Guidelines* for Wildlife Encounters

*Disclaimer: Following these guidelines in no way guarantees your safety. Also, some experts offer different guidelines, but those included here represent the advice most commonly given by multiple sources.

All Animals	Never sneak up on an animal. If you see it before it sees or smells you, get away or make your presence known and give it a wide berth. Formulate an escape plan before reaching for the camera. Restrain your dog unless you consider her sacrificial. Wild animals may be starving in spring. A hungry predator might leave you alone if you throw it the apple it smells in your lunch sack, but don't electively feed wild animals. An unafraid wild animal may be rabid. Warn others. Report predator sightings to local authorities. Do not go near a carcass. A predator may be guarding its kill.
Bear *(In Utah, just black bears)*	Bears are secretive. A bear may warn that you are too close by running towards you, making blowing noises, and swatting the ground. Slowly back away. Don't turn your back to the bear. If it follows, change directions. If it still follows, make yourself look big by putting something over your head. Act aggressive. If it attacks, fight back any way you can. Bear spray is an option but you have to be close and upwind to use it.
Bobcat or **Cougar** *(a.k.a. Puma, Mountain lion)*	 Cougar The cougar is a protected carnivore that hunts at night, but also when deer feed at dawn and dusk. Like most cats, cougars like to ambush or chase fast moving prey. So does the smaller bobcat. DO NOT RUN; you'll look like prey. Make yourself look big with arms, or pack overhead, but if you have to bend to pick up a little child or dog, maintain eye contact with the cougar while you bend. Yell and scream at it. Throw rocks. Fight back if attacked. Do not play dead.
Coyote	 Easily confused with dogs and wolves, coyotes may hunt in packs or alone, mostly at night. They can be a threat to small pets or children. If a wild looking dog is eyeing your little dog, pick your dog up and make yourself big and loud. Fight back in the unlikely event of an attack.
Deer Elk *and* **Moose**	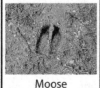 Moose These animals are vegetarian, unlike the predators above. However, they can kick or butt you into smithereens if they think you're a threat. Stay far away. Slowly back away. Moose are the most easily provoked. If one lowers its head it may charge. Hide behind a tree if you can't get away. You can't outrun these animals but they don't have a lot of motivation to chase you. If you can't safely get away, drop and curl into a ball and lie still, protecting your head. Play dead.

PHOTOS by Wikimedia Commons

Please see the chapter on hiking with dogs regarding the management of unfortunate encounters with **porcupines** and **skunks**.

I will confess to readers that in all the years I've hiked in Park City, I never had a really scary wildlife encounter until September 18, 2017, when I had the most terrifying experience of my life. On a familiar neighborhood trail, a mad mama moose suddenly appeared directly in front of me, charging. There was no time to get behind a tree or even back away. I barely had time to turn sideways and drop, covering my head with hands and arms. With forehead to my knees to protect face, chest and abdomen, and a wide brimmed hat, I could not see the moose, but I could smell and feel her standing over me. Motionless, I held my breath and braced for the kicks. She circled around and sniffed me. My heart fluttered until I finally sensed she had moved away and I could exhale.

Still I was afraid to move. I stayed curled up like a snail until I dared to lift my head and see Mama munching on leaves about 10 yards (9 m) away, with her gigantic baby nearby. Slowly, I brought my right hand down. Mrs. Moose didn't notice. I had an urgent goal: to turn off the electronic dance music coming from the phone in my pocket.

I had turned the music on just a few minutes before because I was alone and another hiker had told me she saw the pair. I thought the music would scare them away. Now I wonder if the music irritated Mama, and that's why she charged me. Or, was I just one too many hikers interrupting her lunch? There had been a mild earthquake that morning. Had that put her on edge? Fortunately, turning the music off didn't faze her.

After a few more minutes of sitting like a statue, I found the courage to inch up, back away, and wobble on shaking legs back to the trailhead. A few weeks later, another hiker on another trail was seriously injured by a moose.

Hiking around Park City, I always took comfort in the idea that animals tend to stay away from people-populated trails, especially midday. People noise usually makes them retreat. If you give a moose a wide berth, as opposed to trying to stick a camera in its face, it will usually leave you alone. But none of that applied to this experience, while retrospectively this encounter was avoidable.

When the other hiker told me about the moose pair on this autumn day, I should have reversed course. Moose are most likely to be aggressive in autumn and when mothers are protecting babies. I think the reason I didn't retreat was that I wanted to see the moose. I had come to mistake them for nice neighbors. Moose occasionally visit my backyard and I've met some on trails, ski slopes, and the Muni golf course (pictured here). None were hostile. Once, to my horror, my little girl dachshund rubbed noses with a young cow moose that came alongside the trail. Fortunately, this nasal affair ended well, and I probably came to trust moose a little too much.

In recent years, moose have become regular visitors to neighborhoods all around Park City, where they dine on landscaping. They've also been seen roaming school grounds and walking down Main Street, looking shabby after a harsh winter. Park City's woodlands have become too mature to  provide them with low branches, and too eroded by people building deeper into the forests. An 800-pound moose that has to forage all day to keep warm and nourish a fetus or two during winter, has to eat about 70 pounds (32 kg) of vegetation a day to obtain a needed 10,000 calories. When the canopies of mature tress prevent the growth of new ones, moose turn to the vegetation planted in people's yards, and that grow in the sparse sunlight along trails. As their habitat shrinks, more human-moose encounters may occur.

Or maybe the moose will move on. Moose have not always lived in Utah. In the 1950s, only about 100 moose were thought to have lived here. Today, the state moose population may number 5,000. Moose migrated from Wyoming to Park City in the latter half of the 1900s when local forests were recovering from prior voracious harvesting for timber and fuel. Unless fire creates new-growth forests in Park City, moose may have to go elsewhere to do their special form of tree pruning, which creates healthy forests.

I'll never know why Mama Moose didn't stomp me into pulp. Perhaps her charge was just a warning. Maybe she didn't want to dull her razor-sharp hooves on the pile of rocks I had collapsed into. Maybe she liked the electronic dance music blaring from my phone. Maybe she decided I wasn't a threat because I knew what to do; or I was just very lucky.

The point is, if you hike, you need to know something about the animal residents in whose neighborhoods you trespass, and how best to avoid and deal with close encounters of a wild kind. For certain, I will never again ignore a wildlife warning from another hiker. And, if I suspect there's nearby wildlife when hiking alone, I'll just talk or sing, rather than play music that impedes my hearing and can't readily be turned off. But, I'll continue to hike and relish the opportunity to occasionally see moose.

Please don't be discouraged about hiking because wildlife encounters are possible. Considering that many Park City trail users enjoy wildlife sightings almost daily, the risk of a mishap is extremely small. Just know what to do if it happens to you.

Using This Guidebook

The **hikes** in this guidebook are all located within the greater Park City area.

Approximate Location of the Hikes

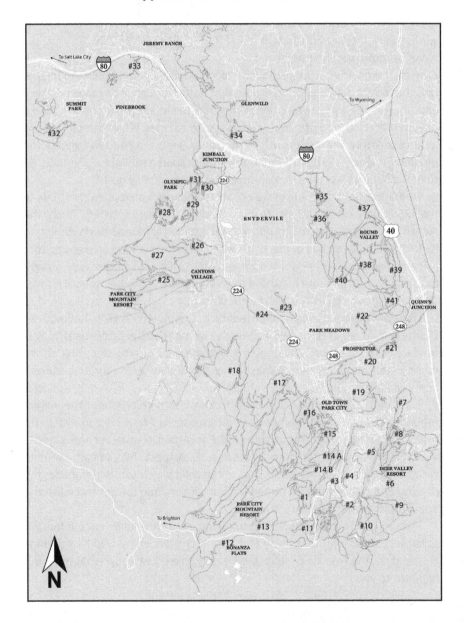

Map Legend

————————	Paved Roads
••••••••••••••••••••••••	Dirt Roads / Maintenance Roads
- - - - - - - - - - - -	Trails
×—×—×—×—×—×—×—×—×—×	Downhill Biking **ONLY** Trails
----------------------	Ski Lifts
- - - - - ▶ - - - - -	Route Direction
∿∿∿	Streams / Rivers
◗	Ponds / Lakes
△	Mountain Tops / Hill Tops
⊤⊤ 👓	Lookout / Scenic View
◯	Bus Stops
🚌	Transit Centers
Ⓟ	Parking
⛳	Golf Courses

	HIKE	**	Dist. mi	Elev. Gain ft
			Hikes by Group* with Distance, Elevation Gain,	
1.	**Empire Pass - Park City Mountain^**	I	**8.8**	**775**
2.	Empire Pass - Silver Lake^	E	2.2	120
3.	**Empire Pass - Ontario Bypass^**	I	**4.6**	**139**
4.	Silver Lake - The Lookout	E	3.0	16
5.	**Silver Lake - Tour De Homes^**	E	**2.7**	**23**
6.	Silver Lake - Deer Crest^	E	4.2	433
7.	**Solamere - Snowtop**	I	**3.6**	**614**
8.	Gap Loop - Route A	I	2.6	340
	Gap- Pipeline - Route B^	I	4.1	634
9.	**Sultan Loop^**	D	**3.2**	**775**
10.	Ontario Canyon - Silver Lake Loop^	D	5.0	1,100
11.	**Red Cloud - Corvair^**	I	**5.3**	**738**
12.	Bloods Lake	E	3.0	495
13.	**9K - Jupiter Ridge^**	D	**5.8**	**1,202**
14A.	Trapper's Loop - Ontario Ridge	I	1.8	311
14B.	Prospect - Empire Link^	D	4.3	912
15.	**Sweeney Switchbacks - 4:20^**	D	**3.7**	**887**
16.	Jenni's - Treasure Hill^	I	5	885
17A.	**Armstrong - Dawns - Routes A^**	I	**3.9**	**840**
17B.	**Armstrong - Dawns - Routes B^**	I	**4.5**	**811**
18.	Iron Mountain^	D	7.8	1,942
19.	**Masonic - Gambel Oak**	I	**4.2**	**577**
20.	Lost Prospector - SOS	I	3.7	700
21.	**Skid Row - Euston**	I	**4.4**	**584**
22.	PC Hill	I	3.3	536
23.	**Quarry Mountain**	D	**3.2**	**685**
24.	McPolin Farm Nature Trail	E	1.7	195
25.	**Holly's^**	D	**4.8**	**953**
26.	Dubois - Collins	I	3.1	650
27.	**Rob's - Rosebud's Heaven^**	D	**7.2**	**1,560**
28.	Yeti's - Moose Puddle	I	6.5	1,190
29.	**Olympic Park Loop**	I	**2.6**	**480**
30A.	Happy Puppy - Down Dog - Route A	E	1.3	138
30B.	Happy Puppy - Down Dog - Route B	E	1.8	194
31.	**RTS**	E	**2.3**	**262**
32.	Road to WOS - Over Easy	D	4.4	1,172
33.	**Gorgoza - Cedar Ridge**	E	**2.6**	**336**
34.	Glenwild - Black Hawk	I	3.0	336
35.	**Trailside Park Loop**	E	**1.1**	**110**
36.	McLeod Creek - Happy Gillmor	E	4.3	420
37.	**RV Connect - Silver Quinns**	E	**3.3**	**289**
38.	Valderoad - Somewhere Elks	I	5.6	526
39.	**Rambler - Kari's**	E	**3.1**	**228**
40.	Matt's Flat - Cammy's	E	2.4	343
41.	**Hat Trick - Ability Way**	E	**2.2**	**206**

^ Not Accessible During Ski Season
**E = Easy   I = Intermediate   D = Difficult
Note: The hikes are divided into 5 groups according to location and other features.

Degree of Difficulty**, and Peak Elevation

Peak Elev. ft	Dist. km	Elev. Gain m	Peak Elev. m	Pg. #
8,650	**14.2**	**236**	**2,637**	**30**
8,170	3.5	37	2,490	34
8,493	**7.4**	**42**	**2,589**	**36**
8,066	4.8	4.9	2,459	39
8,170	**4.4**	**7**	**2,490**	**42**
8,238	6.8	132	2,511	44
7,568	**5.8**	**187**	**2307**	**47**
7,564	4.2	104	2,306	49
7,529	6.6	193	2,295	
8,298	**5.1**	**236**	**2,529**	**52**
9,043	8	335	2,756	54
8,970	**8.5**	**225**	**2,734**	**56**
9,604	4.8	151	2,927	59
9,983	**9.3**	**336**	**3,015**	**61**
7,764	2.9	95	2,366	64
8,162	6.8	278	2,488	66
7,929	**6**	**270**	**2,417**	**69**
7,802	8	270	2,378	72
7,668	**5.8**	**254**	**2,337**	**75**
7,652	8.4	244	2,327	
8,479	12.6	592	2,584	78
7,546	**6.8**	**176**	**2,307**	**81**
7,230	6	213	2,204	84
7,238	**7.1**	**178**	**2,206**	**87**
7,170	5.2	163	2,185	90
7,371	**5.2**	**209**	**2,247**	**93**
6,863	2.7	59	2,092	95
7,737	**7.7**	**290**	**2,358**	**97**
6,683	5	198	2,037	101
7,874	**11.5**	**476**	**2,400**	**103**
8,033	10.5	363	2,448	106
7,422	**4.2**	**146**	**2,262**	**109**
6,698	2.1	42	2,042	113
6,698	2.9	59	2,042	
6,763	**3.6**	**80**	**2,016**	**115**
8,524	7.1	357	2,598	117
6,736	**4.2**	**102**	**2,053**	**120**
7,422	4.8	102	2,044	122
6,690	**1.8**	**34**	**2,039**	**124**
6,890	6.8	128	2,100	126
6,864	**5.3**	**88**	**2,092**	**129**
7,132	9	160	2,430	131
6,932	**5**	**69**	**2,113**	**134**
7.083	3.8	105	2,159	137
6,829	**3.5**	**63**	**2,101**	**140**

*1-6 Bus Up to Deer Valley Resort and Hike Down
7-11 More Deer Valley
12-24 Park City, Park City Mountain, Bonanza Flats

25-35 Canyons, Snyderville Basin
36-41 Round Valley

Group I Hikes #1-6 ~ Bus Up and Hike Down from Deer Valley Resort

These six one-way hikes provide an opportunity to tour the forests of higher elevations with little climbing, by utilizing summer **bus** service to the upper levels of Deer Valley Resort at Empire Pass and Silver Lake. When buses are not in service, hikers will need cars at both hike ends to avoid strenuous uphill walking back to start. Parking is limited, so buses are the best option when available. Having a friend or driver service drop you off is another option.

Four of these hikes take advantage of *Mid Mountain Trail,* the crown jewel of Park City's trail system. This manicured single-track spans 23 miles (37 km) of resort terrain at about 8,000-foot (2,438 km) elevation. It can be busy at peak times. With the exception of hike #4, these routes are not accessible during ski season, and all are usually too snowy and muddy to hike in early spring.

Don't assume downhill hiking is effortless. Unaccustomed participants might experience DOMS (Delayed Onset Muscle Soreness) of the thighs and calves. The high elevation of these hikes can tax the fitness and altitude acclimatization of lowlanders.

Group II Hikes #7-11 ~ More Deer Valley

Six hikes in this group take you around the top, middle and bottom of Deer Valley Resort as it stretches from Park City Mountain Resort to the west, and the Jordanelle Reservoir to the east. For hikes #7 and #8, bus service may be available year-round. Summer bus service is the best option for hikes #9, #10, and #11. All of these hikes are inaccessible during ski season except for #7 and #8A.

Deer Valley Resort, famous for luxury accommodations and as an Olympic ski venue, is also a mecca for summer biking and hiking. Lift assisted access to higher elevations and guided hiking tours are available. See *deervalley.com.*

Group III Hikes #12-24 ~ Park City, Park City Mountain, Bonanza Flats

A vast trail network intimately connects the town of Park City and Park City Mountain Resort. Open space in Bonanza Flats atop Park City Mountain was acquired in 2017.

The fourteen routes included in this group take hikers through ski terrain and the mountains that surround Park City and its suburbs. Park City Mountain, also an Olympic venue, offers lift assisted hiking and biking in summer, and numerous other amenities. *www.parkcitymountain.com*

Group IV Hikes #25-35 ~ Canyons, Snyderville Basin:

Suburban expansion from Park City into the Snyderville Basin has been graced with trail expansion and superb trail maintenance. These twelve routes within local neighborhoods, the Canyons, Swaner Nature Preserve, and Utah Olympic

Park provide a sampling of the variety of landscapes found just north of Park City. *basinrecreation.org*

Group V. Hikes #36-41 ~ Round Valley

Preserved open space at the northeast corner of suburban Park City is home to the Round Valley recreation area. This guidebook takes you on six hiking routes from five different access points through this nearly 700-acre park of interconnecting trails. Many Round Valley trails were designated **leash-free** for hiking dogs on a trial basis in 2016. Hopefully good behavior on the part of dog owners will preserve this privilege. Please heed signs. In spring, when there's still snow in the mountains to the west, Round Valley trails to the east may be warm and dry. Some Round Valley trails are groomed in winter.

Where to Find Winter Trail Info

Park City Municipal
parkcity.org/departments/open-space-and-trails/winter-trails

Mountain Trails Foundation
map.mountaintrails.org/

Basin Recreation
basinrecreation.org/trail conditions

All Hikes

The hikes selected for inclusion in this guidebook are just some of the many routes that could be chosen from the hundreds of miles of trails in and around the greater Park City area. Seven of the hikes in the first edition of this book have been replaced due to impairment of access by reduced parking or construction, or due to a high level of cyclist traffic. The hikes herein are named after their trails or their general locations. Some trail names like *Rambler* and *Mid Mountain* come up repeatedly because these trails cover a vast area and serve as connectors to other trails. *Trail names* in the text *are italicized* to distinguish them from roads and other labels. Trail names used in this guidebook are in accordance with maps produced by Park City's Mountain Trails Foundation.

Many of the hikes in this guidebook are accessible by Park City's **free public bus system**. Bus schedules and routes vary from season to season. Only certified service animals are allowed to accompany humans on buses. Buses are equipped to carry wheelchairs, strollers and a limited number of bicycles. Although the bus is often the best option, parking information is available for all hikes. Unfortunately, **parking is limited**, and parking in an unauthorized place

Where to Find Bus Info

At *www.parkcity.org*
On signs at bus stops
By calling 435-615-5301
On brochures inside buses

often results in towing, significant expense, and more aggravation than that parking spot was worth.

Distances and **elevations are approximate.** They were computed using the smart phone app, *www.mapmywalk.com,* which produces slightly different readings each time I record the same hike. Fractions and metric equivalents are rounded off. If you track these same hikes using any GPS app, your readings will likely differ.

Degree of Difficulty assigned to these hikes is relative only to Park City's mountainous terrain and an individual hiker's fitness. Hiking here invariably involves going up and down, and uphill hiking significantly increases energy expenditure. Trails in this guidebook that are rated difficult may seem easy to a well-conditioned local. They feature longer and/or steeper climbs than hikes that ascend more gently. Trails rated as easy may seem difficult to a lowlander who's used to flatter terrain.

On the following page is another look at the hikes in order of distance to help you select hikes that are within your stamina level and time budget.

Configurations include loops, out-and-backs, one-ways (taking a bus up and hiking down), and lollipops, which are loops with an out-and-back trail access.

Maps of the hikes in this guide identify bus stops, parking areas, and other landmarks where applicable.

Time estimates for each hike are not given. Uphill miles usually take longer than downhill miles. I average 35 min/mile (1.6 km) uphill and 25 min/mile (1.6 km) downhill, but I step aside for cyclists and stop to talk to people, take pictures and pet dogs. You may need less or more time. Each hiker should learn their own pace in order to make reasonable time accommodations for chosen hikes, including time to access and return. Responsible hikers pace themselves at the rate of the slowest hiker in their group.

NOTICE: Trails, paths, roads and landmarks identified on maps or in directions in this book may change. Bus routes and stops may also change. New property ownership, construction, or phenomena such as a rockslide may delete or reroute any of these hikes. Street signs and trail markers may not always be present, may be outdated, and occasionally they get twisted around to point the wrong way. Maps on GPS satellite systems, as well as maps in this book, may lag behind changes in roads and trails. **Please respect barricades and signs indicating Private Property** or **No Trespassing.**

Hikes in Order of Distance with Degree of Difficulty*, Elevation Gain, and Peak Elevation

#	HIKE	*	Dist. mil.	Elev. Gain ft	Peak Elev. ft	Dist. km	Elev. Gain m	Peak Elev. m	Pg. #
35	Trailside Park Loop	E	1.1	110	6,690	1.8	34	2,039	124
30A	Happy Puppy - Down Dog	E	1.3	138	6,698	2.1	42	2,042	113
24	McPolin Farm Nature Trail	E	1.7	195	6,863	2.7	59	2,092	95
30B	Happy Puppy - Down Dog	E	1.8	194	6,698	2.9	59	2,042	113
14A	Trappers Gate - Ontario Ridge	I	1.8	311	7,764	2.9	95	2,366	64
2	Empire Pass - Silver Lake	E	2.2	120	8,170	3.5	37	2,490	34
41	Hat Trick - Ability Way	E	2.2	206	6,892	3.5	63	2,101	140
31	RTS	E	2.3	262	6,763	3.6	80	2,016	115
40	Matt's Flat - Cammy's	E	2.3	343	7.083	3.8	105	2,159	137
8A	Gap Loop	I	2.6	340	7,564	4.2	104	2,306	49
29	Olympic Park Loop	I	2.6	480	7,422	4.2	146	2,262	109
33	Gorgoza - Cedar Ridge	E	2.6	336	6,736	4.2	102	2,053	120
5	Silver Lake - Tour De Homes	E	2.7	23	8,170	4.4	7	2,390	42
4	Silver Lake - The Lookout	E	3.0	16	8,066	4.75	4.9	2,459	39
34	Glenwild - Black Hawk	I	3.0	336	7,422	4.8	102	2,044	122
12	Bloods Lake	E	3.0	495	9,604	4.8	151	2,927	59
26	Dubois - Collins	I	3.1	650	6,683	5.0	198	2,037	101
39	Rambler - Kari's	E	3.1	228	6,932	5.0	69	2,113	134
23	Quarry Mountain	D	3.2	685	7,371	5.2	209	2,247	93
9	Sultan Loop	D	3.2	775	8,298	5.1	236	2,529	52
22	PC Hill	D	3.3	536	7,170	5.2	163	2,185	90
37	RV Connect - Silver Quinns	E	3.3	289	6,864	5.3	88	2,092	129
15	Sweeney Switchbacks - 4:20	D	3.7	887	7,929	6	270	2,417	69
20	Lost Prospector - SOS	I	3.7	700	7,230	6.0	213	2,204	84
17A	Armstrong - Dawns	I	3.9	840	7,668	5.8	254	2,337	75
6	Silver Lake - Deer Crest	E	4.2	433	8,238	6.8	132	2,511	44
19	Masonic - Gambel Oak	I	4.2	577	7,546	6.8	176	2,307	81
14B	Prospect - Empire Link	D	4.3	912	8,162	6.8	278	2,488	66
36	McLeod Creek - Happy Gilmor	I	4.3	420	6,890	6.84	128	2,100	126
7	Solamere - Snowtop	I	4.4	614	7,568	7.1	187	2307	47
21	Skid Row - Euston	I	4.4	584	7,238	7.1	178	2,206	87
32	Road to WOS - Over Easy	D	4.4	1,172	8,524	7.1	357	2,598	117
17B	Armstrong - Dawns	I	4.5	811	7,652	8.4	244	2,327	75
8B	Gap - Pipeline	I	4.5	634	7,529	7.2	193	2,295	49
3	Empire Pass - Ontario Bypass	I	4.6	139	8,493	7.4	42	2,831	3
16	Jenni's - Treasure Hill	I	5.0	885	7,802	8	270	2,378	72
25	Holly's	D	5.0	1,050	7,762	8.0	320	2,366	97
10	Ontario Canyon - Silver Lake Lp.	D	5.0	1,100	9,043	8.0	335	2,756	54
11	Red Cloud - Corvair	I	5.3	738	8,970	8.5	225	2,734	56
38	Valderoad - Somewhere Elks	I	5.6	526	7,132	9.0	160	2,430	131
13	9K Trail - Jupiter Ridge	D	5.8	1,202	9,893	9.3	336	3,015	61
28	Yeti's - Moose Puddle	I	6.5	1,190	8,033	10.5	363	2,448	103
27	Rob's - Rosebud Heaven	D	7.2	1,560	7,874	11.5	476	2,400	103
18	Iron Mt	D	7.8	1,942	8,479	12.6	592	2,584	78
1	Empire Pass - Park City Mtn	I	8.8	775	8,650	14.2	236	2,637	30

*E = Easy   I = Intermediate   D = Difficult

#1 Empire Pass - Park City Mountain

DESCRIPTION: The longest route in this book, this mostly downhill hike along the *Mid Mountain Trail* spans deep shady forests and features a perfusion of alpine flowers and expansive panoramas. Enjoy a tour of the ski terrain of two resorts, with some lookout benches along the way.

Distance: 8.8 miles (14.2 km)

Elev. Gain: 775 feet (236 m)

Peak Elev: 8,650 feet (2,637 m)

Difficulty: *Intermediate*. It would be easy except it's long and there's a big climb for the first few hundred yards.

Configuration: One-way. Bus up and hike down.

Note: Not accessible in ski season.

◊ **Park City Resort** features a multilevel plaza with lodging, dining and shopping. Summer features include an alpine slide, alpine coaster, zip line, lift assisted hiking and cycling, horseback riding, miniature golf, a climbing wall, and other amusement park activities.

DIRECTIONS:

- Ride the Empire Pass bus from the Old Town Transit Center to the Montage Hotel and Empire Canyon Lodge **bus stop**. The bus is the best option when available.

- **Drivers** might find parking to the left of Marsac Avenue, just after the horseshoe turn above the Montage Hotel traffic circle, but only if planning to take the bus back, or leave a second car at Park City Mountain Resort, or walk uphill back to Empire Pass. From parking, walk down Marsac Avenue to the traffic circle bus stop.

- From the Montage bus stop, walk uphill between the buildings on a dirt road. Pass the hotel and find a single-track trail to the right, before the Empire Express Chairlift.

- Turn right onto this single-track, the *Mid Mountain Trail*. Ignore a right fork to *Little Chief Trail,* and proceed to an X-intersection with the *T&G Trail*.
- Cross *T&G Trail* to continue on *Mid Mountain.* Ignore turns to *Link Trail* and come to a fork.
- Bear right and cross a trail under a power line. Proceed to a four-way X-intersection.
- Bear right and proceed to a three-way intersection at a horseshoe turn.
- Bear left and come to a dirt road.
- Turn left onto the road and quickly arrive at a right turn back onto *Mid Mountain Trail*.
- Turn right and cross the road again. Come to a fork with *Tommys Two Step Trail*.
- Bear right to stay on *Mid Mountain.* Cross a ski slope and bear right in the direction *of Jenni's Trail.* Proceed parallel to the Bonanza chairlift and follow *Mid Mountain* to a dirt road.
- Turn sharply left onto the road, proceed a short way, and find the single-track of *Mid Mountain Trail* on the right.
- Turn right and proceed across ski slopes, under the Crescent chairlift, and across more ski slopes. After crossing under the King Con chairlift, come to a three-way intersection.
- Turn sharply right and proceed on *Mid Mountain Trail* to a multi-trail intersection.
- Turn right onto the *CMG Trail.* Continue downhill and come to a three-way intersection.
- Bear left across a road onto *Eagle Trail.* Follow through switchbacks to a three-way intersection.
- Bear right onto the *Spiro Trail.* Proceed through more switchbacks to a four-way intersection.
- Turn right onto the *Silver Spur Trail.* Follow it to any of the trails or dirt roads going down to the base of Park City Mountain. The transit center, or your second car is in front (east) of the resort plaza.

ROUTE SUMMARY:

o From the Montage Hotel bus stop, take the dirt road uphill to a single-track trail on the right, before the chairlift.

o Turn right onto the *Mid Mountain Trail.* Ignore a fork.
Proceed to a four-way intersection.

o Proceed straight across the *T&G Trail.* Ignore turns to *Link Trail,* and proceed to a fork.

o   Bear right and cross a trail under a power line. Proceed to a four-way X-intersection.

o   Bear right and proceed to a three-way intersection at a horseshoe turn.

o   Bear left and come to a road.

o   Turn left and quickly turn right back onto *Mid Mountain Trail*. Come to a fork.

o   Bear right to stay on *Mid Mountain* going towards *Jenni's Trail*. Proceed parallel to a chairlift and come to a dirt road.

o   Turn sharply left onto the road, proceed a short distance, and quickly turn right back onto the single-track of *Mid Mountain Trail*. Come to a three-way intersection

o   Turn sharply right and proceed on *Mid Mountain Trail* to a multi-trail intersection.

o   Turn right onto *CMG Trail*. Continue downhill to a three-way intersection.

o   Bear left onto the *Eagle Trail* and follow it to a three-way intersection.

o   Bear right onto the Spiro Trail and proceed to a four-way intersection.

o   Turn right onto the *Silver Spur Trail* and follow it back to the base of Park City Mountain Resort.

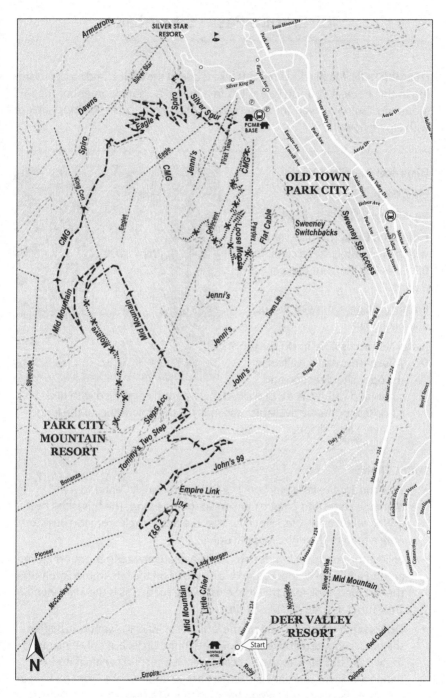

#1 Empire Pass - Park City Mountain

#2 Empire Pass - Silver Lake

DESCRIPTION: Mostly downhill, this hike is one of the easiest and most rewarding in this book, if you use Park City's free buses. A short segment of the Mid Mountain Trail takes you through mature forest and across ski slopes ablaze with alpine flowers.

Distance: 2.2 miles (3.5 km)

Elev. Gain: 120 feet (37 m)

Peak Elev: 8,500 feet (2,591 m)

Difficulty: Easy. This hike starts with a moderately steep climb for 0.2 miles (0.3 km), but the rest is downhill.

Configuration: One-way. Bus up and hike down.

Note: Not accessible in ski season.

◊   This route is easily walked in the opposite direction and combined with walk #1, or walked this way and combined with hikes #3-6. Restrooms are available seasonally in the downstairs of the lodge at Silver Lake Village.

DIRECTIONS:

- Take the Empire Pass bus from the Old Town Transit Center to the Montage Hotel and Empire Canyon Lodge **bus stop**. The bus is the best option when available. Directly across the traffic circle from the bus stop, note a road to the right, looping uphill.

- Follow this road as it bends and climbs a relatively steep but short incline around a horseshoe bend. Ignore a dirt road on the left. Immediately after the dirt road, look for a trail that crosses the road. This is the *Mid Mountain Trail*. Turn left onto *Mid Mountain*.

- **Drivers** might find parking on the left side of Marsac Avenue, just after the horseshoe turn above the Montage traffic circle; but only if planning to take the bus back to the first car, or leave a second car at limited parking in Silver Lake, or walk uphill back to Empire Pass. From parking in Empire Pass, walk north along the road to find a single-track trail crossing the road. Turn right onto this single-track, the *Mid Mountain Trail*.

- Follow *Mid-mountain* across ski slopes. Ignore a few intersecting trails. Cross under five chairlifts. Come to a dirt road.
- Turn left onto this road and arrive at the base of the Sterling chairlift. Continue north to Silver Lake Village.
- Turn left between the buildings to get to Royal Street. Find the Silver Lake Village bus stop on the right, or your second car parked at Silver Lake.

ROUTE SUMMARY;
- Pick up *Mid-Mountain Trail* on the east side of Marsac Avenue around a horseshoe bend in the road above the Montage Hotel traffic circle in Empire Pass.
- Follow the trail eastward, across ski slopes and under five chairlifts. Arrive at a dirt road.
- Turn left and descend past the Sterling chairlift to Silver Lake Village to pick up the bus back to Old Town or the car you parked at Silver Lake.

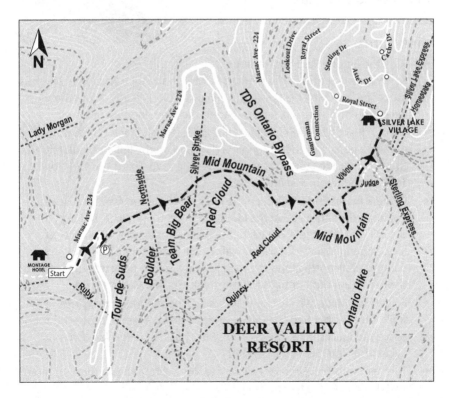

#2 Empire Pass - Silver Lake

#3 Empire Pass - Ontario Bypass

DESCRIPTION: One day in autumn, local cyclists in whacky costumes on crazy bikes will roll down the Ontario Bypass Trail as part of the "Tour De Suds" (TDS), a mountain biking celebration. The rest of the season, hikers can enjoy this route and its antiquities.

Distance: 4.6 miles (7.4 km)

Elev. Gain: 1,439 feet (42 m)

Peak Elev: 8,493 feet (2,589 m)

Difficulty: *Intermediate*. There's a short climb at the start and rocky trail at the end.

Configuration: One-way. Bus up and walk down.

Note: Not Accessible in ski season.

DIRECTIONS:

- Ride the Empire Pass bus from the Old Town Transit Center to the Montage Hotel and Empire Canyon Lodge **bus stop**. The bus is the best option when available. Directly across the traffic circle from the bus stop, note a road to the right, looping uphill.

- Follow this road as it bends and climbs a relatively steep but short incline around a horseshoe bend. Ignore a dirt road on the left. Immediately after the dirt road, look for a trail that crosses the road. This is the *Mid Mountain Trail*. Turn left onto *Mid Mountain*.

- **Drivers** might find parking on the left side of Marsac Avenue, just after the horseshoe turn above the Montage Hotel traffic circle; but only if planning to take the bus back to the first car, or leave a second car at limited parking in Old Town, or walk uphill back to Empire Pass. From parking, walk north along the road to find a single-track trail that crosses the road. Turn right onto the single-track, the *Mid Mountain Trail*.

- Follow *Mid Mountain* eastward across ski slopes. Ignore some intersecting trails. Cross under two chairlifts. Continue down a gentle descent through two switchbacks. After the second switchback, note the *TDS/Ontario Bypass Trail* intersection to the left.

- Turn left onto *TDS/Ontario*. Follow it across a dirt road and through more switchbacks. Come to a fork.

- Bear right and arrive at another fork

- Bear left. Continue through another switchback and descend to Marsac Avenue.
- Carefully cross Marsac and turn right. The *TDS/Ontario Bypass Trail* immediately comes up on the left.
- Turn left onto *TDS/Ontario Bypass* and double-track quickly becomes single-track. Pass the Ontario Mine buildings below you. Continue through several switchbacks following signs for the *Ontario Bypass Trail*. Come to a dirt road.
- Turn left onto this road and quickly come to a curve and single-track trail to the right.
- Turn right onto this ridgeline single-track, *Prospect Trail*, and continue north. This trail becomes rocky and showcases some relics from Park City's historic past. Ignore intersections and the trail will ultimately end on blacktop on Prospect Avenue.
- Walk down this steep narrow street to Hillside Avenue.
- Turn left onto Hillside which ends on the top of Main Street.
- Turn right onto Main Street. Bus riders continue on its east side until you notice a bear statue sitting on a bench to the right.
- Turn right into the walkway just before the bear and arrive on Swede Alley and the Old Town Transit Center or the parking you found in Old Town.

ROUTE SUMMARY:

o   Start on *Mid-Mountain Trail* east of the Montage Hotel. Continue eastward crossing ski slopes and ignoring intersecting trails. Descend through two switchbacks, and note the *TDS/Ontario Bypass Trail* intersection to the left.

o   Turn left onto *Ontario Bypass (Tour De Suds)* and follow it across a dirt road and through more switchbacks. Come to a fork.

o   Bear right and arrive at another fork.

o   Bear left. Continue through another switchback and descend to Marsac Avenue.

o   Cross Marsac and turn right. The *TDS/Ontario Bypass Trail* comes up immediately on the left.

o   Turn left onto *Ontario Bypass*. Continue through several switchbacks following signs for the *TDS/Ontario Bypass Trail*. Come to a dirt road.

o   Turn left and quickly come to a curve and a single-track trail to your right.

o   Turn right onto the single-track and follow it down Prospect Avenue to Hillside Avenue.

o   Turn left onto Hillside and follow it to the top of Main Street.

o   Turn right onto Main Street to return to the Old Town Transit Center.

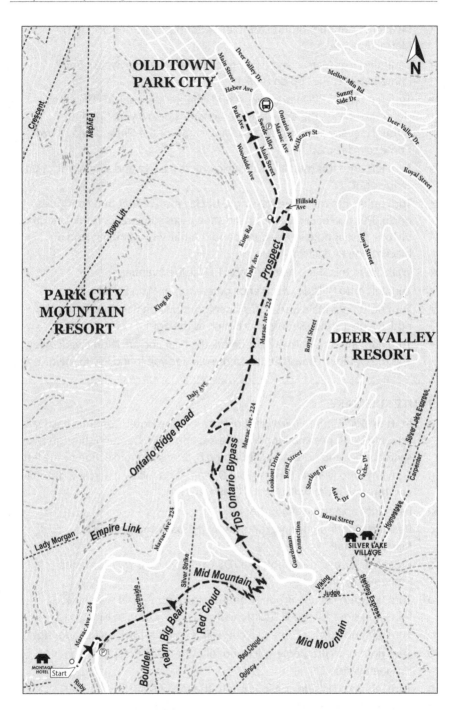

#3 Empire Pass - Ontario Bypass

#4 Silver Lake - The Lookout

DESCRIPTION: Hike downhill from the amenities of Deer Valley Resort to the amenities of Old Town, on shady wooded trails and old mine roads along the east side of Ontario Canyon.

Distance: 3 miles (4.8 km)

Elev. Gain: Just 16 feet (4.9 m)

Peak Elev: 8,066 feet (2,459 m)

Difficulty: *Easy,* though footwork and navigation require attention.

Configuration: One-way. Bus up and hike down.

DIRECTIONS:

- Take the Silver Lake bus from the Old Town Transit Center to the Royal Street and Little Bell Court **bus stop**, just west of Silver Lake Village. **Drivers** can take Marsac Avenue to Guardsman Connection Road and make a right turn onto Royal Street. Very limited parking at Silver Lake Village may be available. If the Silver Lake bus isn't running, you'll need a second car in Old Town or an uphill walk back to Silver Lake.
- From the bus stop or parking, walk west on the sidewalk along Royal Street West until you come to a three-way intersection with Guardsman Connector Road.
- Cross Guardsman Connector and immediately to the left, find *The Lookout Trail.*
- Turn left onto this trail and follow it through five switchbacks. At the third and fifth switchbacks there are forks. Bear right at both. Notice the Ontario Mine complex on the opposite side of the canyon at the fifth switchback. Arrive at a fork.
- Bear left and continue to a three-way intersection with a rock wall on the right.
- Turn sharply left and continue to a fork.
- Bear right and continue to an X-intersection.
- Bear left around a horseshoe turn and arrive at another intersection.
- Continue straight and arrive at another intersection.
- Continue straight again and arrive at a fork.
- Bear left and come to an S-turn. Follow the horseshoes around as indicated by the placement of logs. (No shortcuts please!) Arrive at a fork.

- Bear right where a sign points to *Rossie Hill Trail*. Ignore some stone steps to the left and come to a switchback with a fork.
- Bear right and continue to a three-way intersection.
- Turn left onto double-track and continue to a multi-trail intersection. Look ahead for two low boulders and take the trail just right of the boulders. Proceed, ignoring an intersecting trail to the right, and arrive at another intersecting trail to the right.
- Turn right here and proceed to a paved cul-de-sac, McHenry Avenue.
- Walk north on this street and find a long staircase on your left.
- Take the stairs down and turn right onto Ontario Avenue. Walk north to another long staircase on the left and descend these stairs *(Shortys Steps)* to Marsac Avenue.
- Carefully cross Marsac and take more stairs down through the China Bridge parking structure where you could have left a car, or proceed to Swede Alley and turn right to get to the Old Town Transit Center.

ROUTE SUMMARY:

o   Find the entrance to *The Lookout Trail* on the west side of Royal Street, just north of Guardsman Connection Road.

o   Turn left onto this trail and follow it through five switchbacks, bearing right at switchback forks. Continue to another a fork.

o   Bear left and continue to a three-way intersection.

o   Turn sharply left and continue to a fork.

o   Bear right and continue to an X-intersection.

o   Bear left around a horseshoe turn and arrive at another intersection

o   Continue straight to another intersection.

o   Continue straight again and arrive at a fork.

o   Bear left and come to an S-turn. Follow the horseshoes and come to a fork.

o   Bear right where a sign points to *Rossie Hill Trail,* and come to a switchback with a fork.

o   Bear right and continue to a three-way intersection.

o   Turn left onto double-track and continue to a multi-trail intersection.

o   Take the trail to the right of two low boulders. Ignore an intersecting trail to the right, and arrive at another intersecting trail to the right.

o   Turn right here and proceed to a paved cul-de-sac.

o   Walk north on this street and then down a long staircase on the left.

o   Walk north on this street and take another staircase on the left down to Marsac Avenue.

o   Cross Marsac and take more stairs down through the parking structure where your car could be, or turn right on Swede Alley to get to the Old Town Transit Center.

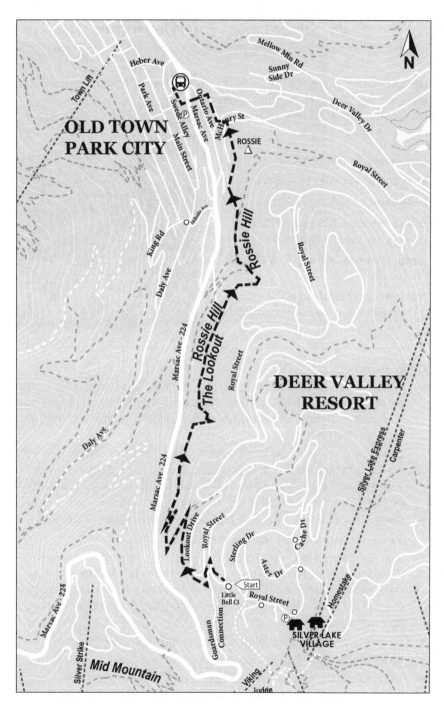

#4 Silver Lake - The Lookout

#5 Silver Lake - Tour De Homes

DESCRIPTION: The natural beauty of Deer Valley ski terrain, coupled with elegant and artsy slope-side estates, makes this route especially entertaining.

Distance: 2.7 miles (4.4 km)

Elev. Gain: A measly 23 feet (7 m)

Peak Elev: 8,170 feet (2,490 m)

Difficulty: *Easy.* Test your altitude tolerance without any climbing.

Configuration: One-way. Bus up and hike down.

Note: Not accessible in ski season.

◊   Construction may reroute this hike. Heed signs.

DIRECTIONS:

- When available, take the Silver Lake bus from the Old Town Transit Center to the Cache Drive and Royal Street **bus stop**. Then walk to the three-way intersection of Royal Street, Cache Drive, and Sterling Drive and turn west onto Sterling Drive.
- **Drivers** could leave a car at the limited parking of Silver Lake, but only if planning to take the bus or walk back, or leave a second car at the Deer Valley Resort base and drive back. From Silver Lake parking, walk north on Royal Street to the second left, Sterling Drive.
- On Sterling, find *Tour De Homes Trail* on the right between residences.
- Turn right onto this trail. Immediately come to a fork.
- Bear right onto a dirt road. Follow it over bridges, through residential developments and under a tunnel. The road turns left and about a mile (1.6 km) from start, it forks right. At times this trail follows single-track to the right of a dirt road, and then veers left back to the road. Arrive at a fork with a single-track.
- Bear right and cross a dirt road. Come to a fork with *Deer Crest Trail.*
- Bear left to stay on *Tour De Homes.* Come to a four-way intersection.
- Turn sharply left and follow the trail under chairlifts to a dirt road.
- Turn left onto this road. Follow it to the Snow Park Lodge, in front of which there's a bus stop and parking on Deer Valley Drive.

ROUTE SUMMARY:

o On the northeast side of Sterling Drive, turn right onto *Tour De Homes Trail* between residences.

o Bear right at a fork onto a dirt road. It diverges right onto single-track and bends left back to the road. Come to a fork with a single-track.

o Bear right. Cross a road and come to a fork with *Deer Crest Trail*.

o Bear left to stay on *Tour De Homes*. Come to a four-way intersection.

o Turn sharply left and follow the trail under chairlifts to a dirt road.

o Turn left onto this road to Snow Park Lodge, the bus stop and parking.

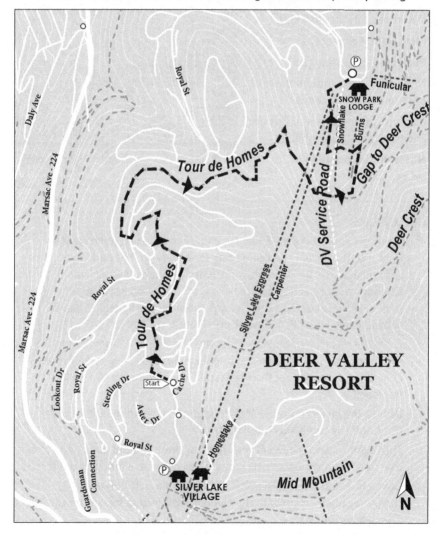

#5 Silver Lake - Tour De Homes

#6 Silver Lake - Deer Crest

DESCRIPTION: If the routes in this book were rated just for the magnificence of their views, this hike overlooking the Jordanelle Reservoir might win first prize. Start with a free bus ride to Silver Lake and follow the gentle grades of the Mid Mountain and Deer Crest Trails downhill to the base of Deer Valley Resort. It's also a great climb if you reverse direction.

Distance: 4.2 miles (6.8 km)

Elev. Gain: 433 feet (132 m)

Peak Elev: 8,238 feet (2,511 m)

Difficulty: *Easy,* though there are some gentle ascents.

Configuration: One-way. Bus up and hike mostly downhill.

Note: Not accessible in ski season.

DIRECTIONS:

- When available, take the Silver Lake bus from the Old Town Transit Center to the Silver Lake Village **bus stop**. Very limited parking at Silver Lake Village may be available for **drivers** who take Marsac Avenue to Guardsman Connection and make a right turn onto Royal Street. If you park in Silver Lake when the bus isn't running, you'll need to leave a second car at Snow Park or walk uphill back to Silver Lake.

- From the bus stop or parking, cross the Silver Lake Village plaza to the ski slopes, bearing left after the buildings. Pass the Silver Lake Express chairlift and cross under the Homestake chairlift. Arrive at a multi-trail intersection.

- Bear to the far left onto the *Mid Mountain Trail* heading uphill. Continue to a three-way intersection.

- Turn right toward the *Deer Crest Trail*. Continue straight as the trail comes to a clearing and crosses a dirt road. Then come to a fork with a dirt road.

- Bear left. Ignore a left turn at the Gnat's Eye ski trail. Come to a three-way intersection with the *Outlook Trail*, (not to be confused with *The Lookout Trail*).

- Turn right and proceed to a fork that quickly triangulates with another fork. Turn left at both onto the *Pipeline Trail*. Proceed through several switchbacks to a three-way intersection.
- Proceed straight through more switchbacks and arrive at another fork with the *Gap To Deer Crest Trail*.
- Turn right. Continue by crossing a dirt road that heads to the St. Regis Hotel. Arrive at a three-way intersection.
- Turn right onto the *Gap Bypass Trail* and proceed to a multi-trail intersection.
- Turn sharply left onto the *Deer Crest Access Trail*. Follow it as it crosses under two chairlifts.
- Turn right onto a dirt road before the third chairlift. This road takes you to the Snow Park Lodge at the base of Deer Valley Resort. Parking and the bus stop are in front (north) of the lodge.

ROUTE SUMMARY:

o   In the midsection of Deer Valley Resort, cross the Silver Lake Village plaza, bearing left. Pass the Silver Lake Express chairlift. Continue under the Homestake chairlift to a multi-trail intersection.

o   Bear far left onto *Mid Mountain Trail*. Follow it uphill to a three-way intersection.

o   Turn right toward *Deer Crest Trail*. Follow it straight across a dirt road. Continue to a fork with another dirt road.

o   Turn left and proceed, ignoring a left turn down a ski slope. Come to a three-way intersection with the *Outlook Trail*.

o   Turn right onto *Outlook* and proceed to a fork that quickly triangulates with another fork. Turn left at both forks onto the *Pipeline Trail*. Proceed to a three-way intersection.

o   Proceed straight. Continue through more switchbacks and arrive at another fork with the *Gap To Deer Crest Trail*.

o   Turn right and cross a dirt road to arrive at a three-way intersection.

o   Turn right onto *Gap Bypass Trail* and proceed to a multi-trail intersection.

o   Turn sharply left onto *Deer Crest Access Trail*. Follow it under two chairlifts. Turn right onto a dirt road before the third chairlift to arrive at Snow Park Lodge, parking and the bus stop.

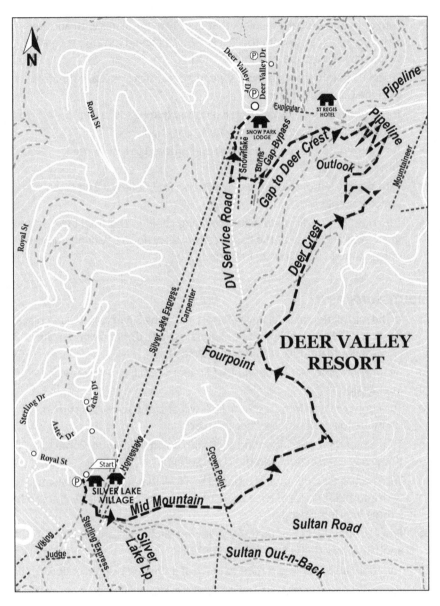

#6 Silver Lake - Deer Crest

#7 Solamere - Snowtop

DESCRIPTION: Maple and chokecherry trees provide a brilliant pallet of autumn colors along this ridgeline hike. A panoramic lookout, duck ponds, and lift-assisted access to additional terrain are nearby.

Distance: 3.6 miles (5.8 km) by bus, 4.4 by car (7.1 km)

Elev. Gain: 614 feet (187 m)

Peak Elev: 7,568 feet (2,307 m)

Difficulty: *Intermediate.* Switchbacks make for gentle grades.

Configuration: Lollipop.

DIRECTIONS:

- Ride the bus to the Queen Esther and Deer Valley Drive **bus stop**, or find **parking** in the northeast corner of the resort lot. Then walk north along Deer Valley Drive East to Queen Esther Drive.
- Bus riders turn left and drivers turn right onto Queen Esther. Find a sign for Deer Crest on the east side of this street, and a footpath to the left of the gated road. Ascend on this path, ignoring an immediate right fork. Arrive at an intersection with the *Solamere Trail*.
- Turn left and continue to a fork.
- Bear right and proceed to a paved cul-de-sac on Hidden Hollow Lane.
- Turn right onto a sidewalk and immediately turn right again onto a single-track, the *Snowtop Trail*. Follow it to a three-way intersection. The rocky trail forking left is a short climb to a recommended lookout **detour**. Descend the same way you came up, turn left, and continue downhill to an intersection.
- At an intersection after the detour, turn right. Come to another intersection.
- Turn left and follow the trail downhill to its end on Queen Esther Drive.
- Turn left for the bus stop. Drivers turn left onto Deer Valley Drive East to return to parking.

ROUTE SUMMARY:

o Find a footpath left of the gated road to Deer Crest on Queen Esther Drive. Take this path, ignoring an immediate right fork. Come to an intersection.

o Turn left and come to a fork.

o Bear right and continue to a paved cul-de-sac.

o Turn right and immediately turn right again back onto single-track. Proceed to a fork. The route continues to the right and comes to an intersection.

o Bear right and come to another intersection.

o Turn left to return to Queen Esther Drive and the bus stop. Drivers turn left on Deer Valley Drive East to return to parking.

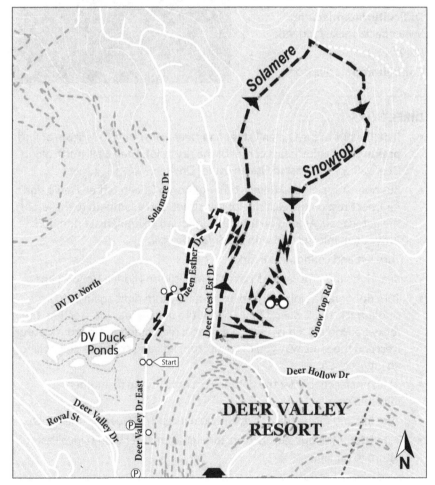

#7 Solamere - Snowtop

#8 Gap - Pipeline

DESCRIPTION: Especially spectacular in autumn, these hikes meander around the magnificent terrain of the Deer Valley and St. Regis Resorts, which offer many other amenities.

Distance: 2.6 or 4.1 miles (4.2 or 6.6 km)

Elev. Gain: 340 or 634 feet (104 or 193 m)

Peak Elev: 7,564 or 7,529 feet (2,306 or 2,295 m)

Difficulty: *Intermediate* with a few gentle climbs.

Configuration: Loops.

Note: Route B is not accessible in ski season.

◊ Both Routes A and B start and end on the same trails but diverge scenically for most of their distance.

◊ Signage here might be outdated. Ignore trail signs that don't jive with these instructions.

◊ The St. Regis funicular is a free public transportation system up and down the hillside between the Snow Park Lodge at the base of Deer Valley Resort and the St. Regis Resort. It can provide a shortcut to and from Route B or be a scenic ride unto itself.

DIRECTIONS (ROUTE SUMMARIES):

- Ride to the Snow Park Lodge **bus stop** at the base of Deer Valley Resort, where **drivers** may find parking. Note the St. Regis Funicular east of Snow Park Lodge.

For both Routes A and B:

- From the bus stop or parking, enter the road that ascends to the St. Regis funicular building. Find *Finn's Trail* to the left, as soon as you turn onto the road.
- Turn left onto *Finn's Trail,* a single-track. Quickly arrive at and ignore a right turn that switches back. Shortly thereafter, come to a three-way intersection.

- Turn sharply right, switching back, and proceed to another three-way intersection.
- Turn left onto *Gap Bypass Trail* and arrive at another three-way intersection.
- Proceed straight. The trail bends east towards paved Deer Crest Estates Drive. Notice a log and stone gatehouse below. Come to a multi-trail intersection above the gatehouse.

Route A - Gap Loop, (the shorter route):

- At the multi-trail intersection above the gatehouse, take the trail to the right, *Gap Loop*, but not the extreme right (also *Gap Loop*). Proceed uphill towards the St. Regis Resort. Switch back just before the hotel. Come to a fork.
- Bear left to continue over the ridge and come to a three-way intersection.
- Turn right, proceed through switchbacks, and come to another three-way intersection.
- Turn left and proceed to another three-way intersection.
- Turn right and come to another three-way intersection.
- Turn left and proceed to a fork.
- Bear right and an intersecting trail quickly comes up on the right.
- Turn right and descend on this trail to a three-way intersection.
- Turn left and the trail returns you to the road to the funicular building.
- Turn right to return to the Snow Park Lodge bus stop or parking.

Route B - Pipeline, (the longer route):

- From the multi-trail intersection above the gatehouse, take the trail to the left going downhill to the paved road. Cross the road and walk uphill. Pass a guardrail and just before a second guardrail, note the *Village Trail* to the left.
- Turn left onto this trail and proceed to a three-way intersection.
- Turn to the extreme left and proceed across a ski slope and across a dirt road. Continue around the bottom of the Mountaineer Express chairlift and bear right onto the *Pipeline Trail*. Arrive at another three-way intersection.
- Turn to the extreme right and proceed to an intersection near a rock wall.
- Turn left to go under the road and merge with a dirt road that loops around the St. Regis Hotel, the *St. Regis Connector Trail*. (You could take the funicular down from here.) If still walking, you'll arrive at a three-way intersection.
- Turn right and come to a dirt road.

- Turn left and find the trail on the right side of the road going downhill. Follow it past the hotel lawn and utility boxes on the left. The *St. Regis Trail* bends around to the right and crosses under the funicular. Come to a fork.
- Bear left. Proceed to a three-way intersection.
- Turn sharply left. Come to a fork.
- Bear right and quickly come to an intersecting trail on the right.
- Turn right and come to a three-way intersection.
- Turn left to exit the trail onto the funicular road and return to start.

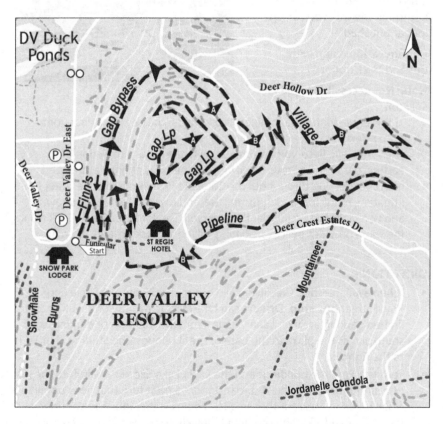

#8 Gap - Pipeline

#9 Sultan Loop

DESCRIPTION: This route through McHenry Canyon starts and ends in Silver Lake Village in the middle of Deer Valley Resort. It offers resort amenities, mining history, and a picnic deck with views of the Jordanelle Reservoir.

Distance: 3.2 miles (5.1 km)

Elev. Gain: 775 feet (236 m)

Peak Elev: 8,298 feet (2,529 m)

Difficulty: *Difficult*. End with a long climb without shade. Returning the way you came is longer but shadier.

Configuration: Loop with out-and-back option.

Note: Not accessible in ski season.

◊ This is equestrian terrain. Hikers must yield to horses. Take directions from riders.

◊ The Jordanelle Reservoir was created with the 1993 completion of an earthen dam on the Provo River. In 1956, the U.S. Congress authorized dam construction throughout the Colorado River Basin to store water for irrigation, municipal and industrial use, and to create power. Two towns and two highways rest under this reservoir. The Jordanelle State Park along the shore provides beaches, boating, hiking, picnicking, and camping.

DIRECTIONS:

- When available, ride the Silver Lake bus to the Silver Lake Drive and Royal Street **bus stop**. **Drivers** can take Marsac Avenue or Royal Street to limited parking at Silver Lake Village. From the bus stop or parking, walk south across the plaza to the base of the ski slopes. The Sterling chairlift is to the right.

- Turn left. Pass the buildings and the Silver Lake Express chairlift to the left of a dirt road. Follow this dirt road. Ignore a right turn that goes uphill to a small building. Pass another small building on the right and continue past two trails that fork right and uphill. Quickly come to a third uphill fork.

- Bear right at the third fork onto single-track into woods, the *Sultan Out-n-Back Trail*. Ignore some uphill forks on the right and proceed across ski slopes and under the Wasatch Express chairlift. The single-track trail sometimes diverges into double-track. Come to an intersecting dirt road.

- Go straight across the road and cross under the Sultan Express chairlift. The trail bends left and merges with a dirt road.
- Bear left onto this road. Ignore a right turn. Proceed to a right fork to the picnic deck/lookout.
- Continue on the dirt road, or turn right onto this road when leaving the lookout. Follow the road around a bend and come to a three-way intersection.
- Turn sharply left onto the dirt *Sultan Road* and begin the uphill climb past the chairlifts and back to the buildings at Silver Lake Village. It's about a 1-mile (1.6 km) climb.
- Turn right between the buildings to return to the bus stop or parking.

ROUTE SUMMARY:

◊   From Silver Lake Village, walk south to the base of the ski slopes.

◊   Turn left and follow a dirt road past two small buildings. Take the third fork to the right after the second building. Ignore some uphill forks and proceed across ski slopes and under a chairlift. Cross a dirt road and under another chairlift. The trail bends left and merges with a dirt road.

◊   Follow this road to the left past the picnic/lookout deck, to a three-way intersection.

◊   Turn sharply left and follow the dirt road back to start.

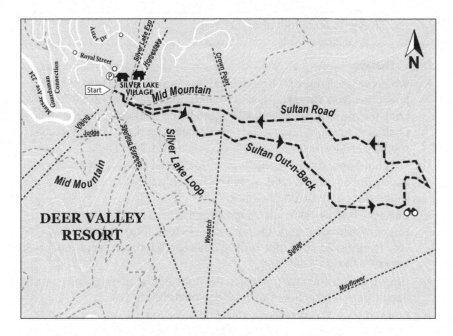

#9 Sultan Loop

#10 Ontario Canyon - Silver Lake Loop

DESCRIPTION: This rewarding route follows hiking-only trails that feature a treasure chest of scenery. Deer Valley Resort amenities are also available.

Distance: 5.0 miles (8 km)

Elev. Gain: 1,100 feet (335 m)

Peak Elev: 9,043 feet (2,756 m)

Difficulty: *Difficult,* but there may be an option to purchase a chairlift ride to the top.

Configuration: Loop.

Note: Not accessible in ski season.

◊ Plaques provide historical information about the New York, Wabash, and Naildriver Mines, which formerly dotted this landscape.

◊ Dead trees have been left to return to earth. Called **glading**, this practice helps support healthier trees.

◊ Consult *deervalley.com* for information about guided hikes, other trails, special events, and other resort activities.

DIRECTIONS:

- When available, ride the Silver Lake bus to the Silver Lake Drive and Royal Street **bus stop. Drivers** may find limited parking at Silver Lake Village. From the bus stop or parking, walk south to the ski slopes. Find the Sterling Chairlift to the right, and ascend the dirt road right of the chairlift. At the third chairlift tower on your left, find a single-track to the right.

- Turn right onto this path, the *Ontario Hike Trail.* It borders the *Homeward Bound Trail* to the left, for downhill cyclists only. Stay to the right until the single-track ends on double-track.

- Cross the double-track, watching for cyclists, and bear left as a single-track enters trees. It gets steeper and rocky for a short distance. Pass a big rock formation on the right and the trail veers left to arrive at a multi-trail intersection with a dirt road.

- Cross the road and take the trail to the right. Pass a reservoir and come to a multi-trail intersection. Watch for downhill cyclists.

- Proceed straight across the intersecting trails onto *Silver Lake Loop Trail,* and switchback up Bald Mountain through fields of sagebrush. Then descend across ski trails to a dirt road.

- Turn left onto the road, pass the Silver Lake Express chairlift on the right, and bear right to arrive at Silver Lake Village for the bus stop or parking.

ROUTE SUMMARY:

o From Silver Lake Village, take the uphill dirt road right of the Sterling chairlift.

o At the third chairlift tower, turn right onto a single-track, the *Ontario Hike Trail*. Cross a double-track trail that bends right to pick up the single-track as it bends left into woods. Continue to a multi-trail intersection with a double-track dirt road.

o Cross the double-track and take the trail to the right. Continue around a reservoir and proceed to a multi-trail intersection.

o Proceed straight onto the *Silver Lake Loop Trail* until it ends on a dirt road.

o Turn left on the road and then bear right to return to start.

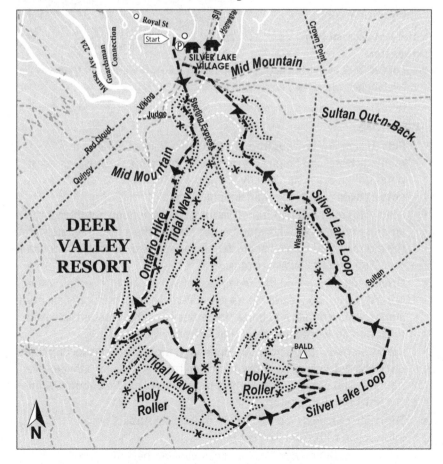

#10 Ontario Canyon - Silver Lake Loop

#11 Red Cloud - Corvair

DESCRIPTION: This hike takes you from the *Mid Mountain Trail* up and around Flagstaff Mountain. It traverses ski terrain amidst the fir-aspen belt of Deer Valley Resort.

Distance: 5.3 miles (8.5 km)

Elev Gain: 738 feet (225 m)

Peak Elev: 8,970 feet (2,734 m)

Difficulty: *Intermediate*. Gentle ascents.

Configuration: Loop.

Note: Not accessible in ski season.

◊ Lots of trees along these trails loop downhill. They were bent that way by avalanches when they were little saplings.

DIRECTIONS:

- Ride the Empire Pass bus from the Old Town Transit Center to the Montage Hotel and Empire Canyon Lodge **bus stop**. The bus is the best option when available. Directly across the traffic circle from the bus stop, note a paved road to the right, looping uphill.

- Follow this road as it bends and climbs a relatively steep but short incline around a horseshoe bend. Ignore a dirt road on the left. Immediately after the dirt road, find a trail that crosses the paved road. This is *Mid Mountain Trail*. Turn left onto *Mid Mountain*.

- **Drivers** might find limited parking east of Marsac Avenue, just after the horseshoe turn above the Montage traffic circle. From parking, walk north along the paved road and find a single-track trail that crosses the paved road. Turn right onto this single-track, the *Mid Mountain Trail*.

- Follow *Mid Mountain* across ski slopes, ignoring several intersecting trails, until after you've passed under two chairlifts. Then look for a trail to the right heading uphill. This is the hiking-only *Red Cloud Trail*, about 0.9 miles (1.4 km) from the bus stop.

- Turn right onto *Red Cloud*. Follow it through switchbacks to an intersection with *Team Big Bear Trail*.

- Proceed straight on *Red Cloud* and come to another intersection.

- Proceed straight. Single-track becomes double-track and briefly turns into a gravel road. Quickly come to another intersection.

- Take the single-track that forks right into the trees. This is the *Moose Bones Trail*. Continue on *Moose Bones*, ignoring a left fork and arriving at another fork with *Boulder Trail*.
- Bear left to stay on *Moose Bones*. When you come to a chairlift and intersection, continue straight, crossing a paved road horseshoe and heading back onto single-track.
- Ignore a left fork. Note a road to your right, but stay on the footpath to the left of the road. Come to another paved road horseshoe.
- Cross the road and pick up the single-track on the opposite side. Follow it to another paved horseshoe. Note a dirt road on the opposite side. The *Corvair Trail* is right of the dirt road.
- Cross the paved road and take the *Corvair Trail*. Quickly come to a fork with *C2T&G Trail*.
- Bear right onto *C2T&G*. Come around a switchback, ignore the *Payroll Trail* for downhill cyclists on the right, and come to a three-way intersection.
- Bear right to return to the *Corvair Trail*.
- Ignore a left fork that connects with the middle of a switchback. Ignore a right fork and come to an X-intersection.
- Veer right at this intersection and follow the switchbacks of the *Corvair Trail* to a three-way intersection with the *Mid Mountain Trail*.
- Turn left onto *Mid Mountain* and come to an intersection with a dirt road.
- Turn right onto this dirt road and come to a fork.
- Bear left and come to an intersection.
- Turn right and continue around the Montage Hotel back to the bus stop or parking.

Route Summary:

o   Turn east onto *Mid Mountain Trail* where it intersects Marsac Avenue above the traffic circle at the Montage Hotel. Ignore intersecting trails until after passing under two chairlifts. Come to an intersection with the *Red Cloud Trail* forking right.

o   Turn right onto *Red Cloud* and follow it to an intersection with *Team Big Bear Trail*.

o   Proceed straight and come to another intersection.

o   Proceed straight. Single-track becomes double-track and briefly turns into a gravel road. Quickly come to another intersection.

o   Take the single-track that forks right. Continue on *Moose Bones Trail*, ignoring a left fork, and arrive at a fork with *Boulder Trail*.

o   Bear left to stay on *Moose Bones*. Continue straight across a paved road back onto single-track. Ignore a left fork. Stay on the footpath left of a paved road. Come to a paved horseshoe.

o Cross the horseshoe and pick up the trail on the opposite side. Continue to another horseshoe. Note a dirt road on the opposite side. *Corvair Trail* is right of the dirt road.

o Take *Corvair Trail*. Quickly come to a fork with *C2T&G Trail*.

o Bear right, ignore a left fork, and come to a three-way intersection.

o Bear right to return to *Corvair Trail*.

o Ignore a fork in the middle of a switchback and then ignore a right fork. Come to an X-intersection.

o Bear right and follow the switchbacks to a three-way intersection with *Mid Mountain Trail*.

o Turn left onto *Mid Mountain* and come to an intersection with a dirt road.

o Turn right onto this road and come to a fork.

o Bear left and come to an intersection.

o Turn right and continue around the Montage Hotel back to start.

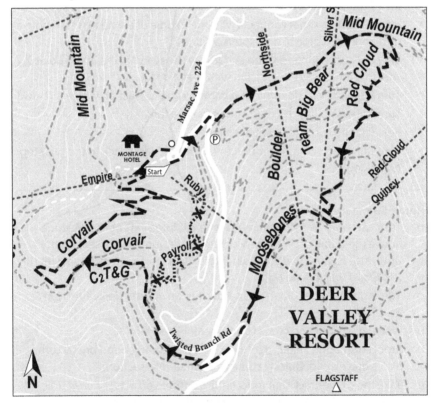

#11 Red Cloud - Corvair

#12 Bloods Lake

DESCRIPTION: This high-altitude, hiking-only route takes you to one of the spring-fed lakes of Bonanza Flats, 1,350 acres purchased by Park City Municipal in 2017 to preserve open space. This conservation area is slated for development of additional trails.

Distance: 3 miles (4.8 km)

Elev. Gain: 495 feet (151 m)

Peak Elev: 9,604 (2,927 m)

Difficulty: Easy

Configuration: Out-and-back.

Note:

◊ **Bus service is not available.** Parking is limited and this hike is extremely popular, especially if it's hot in Salt Lake City. It can be tough to gain access on prime days.

◊ It might be cooler and windier here than in town, 3,000 feet (914 m) below. For those who really like to chill, a swinging rope could be hanging on the lake's south side.

DIRECTIONS (ROUTE SUMMARIES):

▪ There is **no bus** service. **Drivers** take Marsac Avenue south. It becomes Guardsman Pass, (closed if there's snow, possibly late into spring). On the right (north) side of Guardsman, approximately 6.4 miles (11.9 km) from the roundabout intersection of Marsac Avenue and Deer Valley Drive, find the Blood's Lake trailhead parking. Take the second turn into the parking area. There are restrooms in the parking area. Do not park along the road.

▪ Carefully cross Guardsman Road to find the *Bloods Lake Trail*. Proceed on this easy to follow trail to the east side of the lake.

▪ Return to start by following the same trail back to the parking on Guardsman Road.

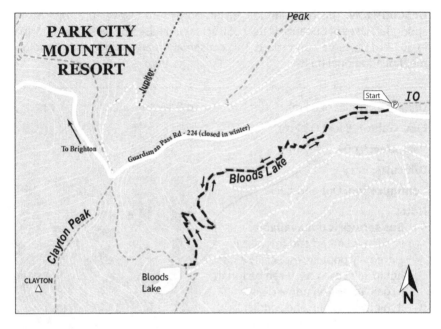

#12 Bloods Lake

#13 9K Trail - Jupiter Ridge

DESCRIPTION: Incredible views and a tour of the expert terrain of Deer Valley and Park City Resorts are featured on this route. Rockhounds will love this terrain, but this route might not be as appealing to people who dislike heights.

Distance: 5.8 miles (9.3 km)

Elev. Gain: 1,202 feet (336 m)

Peak Elev: 9,893 feet (3,015 m)

Difficulty: *Difficult*, wear sturdy shoes.

Configuration: Lollipop.

Note: Not accessible in ski season.

DIRECTIONS:

- There is **no bus** service. **Drivers** take Marsac Avenue south. It becomes Guardsman Pass, (closed if there's snow, possibly late into spring). On the right (north) side of Guardsman, approximately 6.4 miles (11.9 km) from the roundabout intersection of Marsac Avenue and Deer Valley Drive, find the Blood's Lake trailhead parking. Take the second turn into the parking area where you will find restrooms. Do not park on the road.

- At the far (east) end of parking, find the *IO Trail*. Follow it to a dirt road and proceed straight across the road and then onto the dirt road that bends left. Quickly come upon a single-track trail going both ways. This is the *9K Trail*.

- Turn left onto *9K*. Follow it across ski slopes and under the Empire Express Chairlift. Come to a four-way intersection with *Black Forest Trail*.

- Bear left. Come to a five-way intersection. Cross the road staying straight. Come to a fork.

- Bear right and come to a multi-trail intersection.

- Stay left. Ignore a double-track road. Ignore a right turn after crossing under McConkey's Chairlift. The trail gets rocky. Ignore an uphill right turn. Come to a four-way intersection with a dirt road and a sign towards *Apex Trail*.

- Turn left to ascend the rocky road up *Pioneer Ridge*. Go left or right around a small building. Ignore a turnoff called *Perrier Pass*. Ignore another right turnoff to *Apex Trail*. The road bends left and merges with another road. Bear left and quickly find a trail veering off to the right marked "Hiking Only *IO*."

- Turn right onto this trail and follow it along *Jupiter Ridge Trail*. Ignore a left fork. Come to an intersection at the top of the McConkey's Chairlift and make a sharp right hairpin turn onto a dirt road, *Jupiter Hill Road*. Proceed on this road through a left hairpin turn. Ignore a right fork. Ignore a left uphill turn. Come to a multi-trail intersection.

- Stay right. Come to a multi-trail intersection with a dirt road and make a sharp right hairpin turn onto *IO Trail* to return to parking.

ROUTE SUMMARY:

o   Start at the Bloods Lake Trailhead **parking** area on the north side of Guardsman Pass.

o   At the northeast end of parking, take the *IO Trail* to a dirt road. Proceed across the road and onto the dirt road that bends left. Come to a single-track trail going both ways.

o   Turn left onto *9K Trail*. Follow it to a four-way intersection.

o   Bear left. Come to a five-way intersection. Cross the road staying straight. Come to a fork.

o   Bear right and come to a multi-trail intersection.

o   Stay left. Ignore a double-track road and a right turn after the McConkey's Chairlift. Ignore an uphill right turn. Come to a four-way intersection with a dirt road.

o   Turn left to ascend *Pioneer Ridge*. Go left or right around a small building. Ignore two right turnoffs. The road bends left and merges with another dirt road. Turn left and find a trail veering off to the right marked "Hiking Only *IO*."

o   Turn right onto this trail. Ignore a left fork. Come to an intersection at the top of the McConkey's Chairlift and make a sharp right turn onto a dirt road. Proceed through a left hairpin turn. Ignore a right fork. Ignore a left uphill turn. Come to a multi-trail intersection.

o   Stay right. Come to a multi-trail intersection. Turn right 180° onto *IO Trail* to return to start.

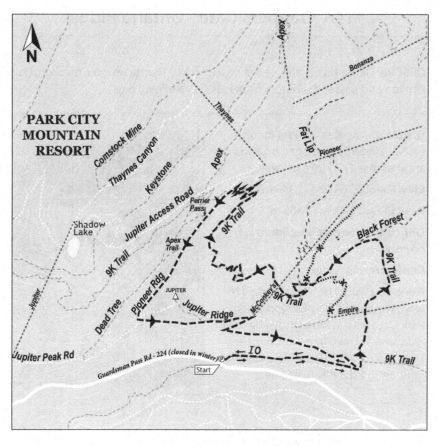

#13 9K Trail - Jupiter Ridge

#14A Trappers Gate - Ontario Ridge

DESCRIPTION: This is the easier of two hikes that takes you through Daly Canyon and past some history from Park City's mining days.

Distance: 1.8 miles (2.9 km) for drivers. Walking from the bus stop adds another mile (1.6 km) each way.

Elev. Gain: 7,764 feet (2,366 m)

Peak Elev: ,764 feet (2,366 m)

Difficulty: *Intermediate,* *bordering on easy.*

Configuration: Loop.

Note: You would not have wanted to walk in beautiful Daly Canyon when Park City was a mining town. *(Photo of Alliance Mine used by permission, Utah Historical Society.)* Hike #14B passes by remnants of the Alliance Mine.

DIRECTIONS (ROUTE SUMMARY):

- Exit the Main Street Trolley at the Hillside and Top of Main **bus stop** and bear left onto Daly Avenue.

- Trolley riders and **drivers** should follow Daly Avenue, an extension of Main Street, south for about a mile (1.6 km). Find limited parking on the left. Proceed south around a gate. Shortly before coming to a small building on the right, find the *Daly Bypass Trail*.

- Turn right onto *Daly Bypass* and come to a fork.

- Bear left onto the *Daily Overlook Trail* and come to a fork.

- Bear extreme left and follow this trail until it ends on a dirt road.

- Cross the road and cross the stream via a rock bridge to get to *Trappers Gate Trail*.

- Bear left onto *Trappers Gate* and come to a fork.

- Bear left and continue to a T-intersection.

- Turn to the extreme right onto historic *Ontario Ridge Trail*. Come to a fork.

- Bear right, proceed up "steps" and come to a fork.

- Bear right and follow the dirt road down and around a water tank. Continue on the dirt road back to start on Daly Avenue.

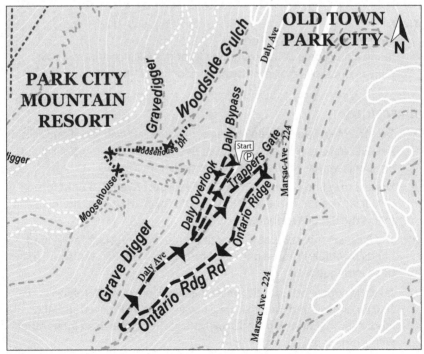

#14A Trappers Gate - Ontario Ridge

#14B Prospect - Empire Link

DESCRIPTION: From Old Town to Deer Valley, these trails are 99.997% user friendly and fantastic. However, for about 25 yards (23 m), you will need to traverse a very high, narrow ledge. This route is definitely not recommended for people who dislike heights. There are also some steps on wooden bridges.

Distance: 4.25 miles (6.8 km) Trolley riders add 1/4 mi. (0.4 km) and a lot of elevation each way.

Elev. Gain: 912 feet (278 m), 1,090 (332 m) by trolley

Peak Elev: 8,162 feet (2,488 m)

Difficulty: *Difficult* due to a steady ascent for the first mile (1.6 km) and some rocky terrain.

Configuration: Lollipop.

Note:
◊ Vestiges of Park City's history are found along some of this route. See what the Alliance Mine and Daly Canyon once looked like in the picture for hike #14A.

DIRECTIONS:

- Take the Main Street **Trolley** to the turnaround at Main Street and Hillside Avenue. Walk up Hillside to Prospect Avenue and turn right. Walking up Prospect Avenue will be the steepest part of the climb.

- **Drivers** may find parking at the top of Prospect Avenue, a right fork off of Marsac Avenue at the south end of Old Town, or park in Old Town and follow the directions above.

- The *Prospect Trail* starts at the top of Prospect Avenue before the road bends downhill. Proceed onto the *Prospect Trail* and follow it south to a three-pronged fork.

- Take the middle branch and arrive at an intersection with *Trappers Gate Trail* forking left and forking right a few feet ahead. Proceed straight. Ignore another right fork and shortly thereafter, come to an intersection with a dirt road.

- Turn left, then quickly turn right onto another dirt road and then immediately turn left to stay on the *Ontario Ridge Trail*. Come to a four-way intersection with the *TDS Ontario Bypass Trail* and proceed straight across it. Come to a three-way intersection.

- Bear right and quickly come to another intersection.
- Bear right onto the *Empire Link Trail*, taking the higher road to the left. Ignore a few left forks. Cross a wooden bridge onto Ontario Ridge Road near the Lady Morgan chairlift. You do have the option of walking down the road, but the prescribed route takes you across the road and back onto the *Empire Link Trail*. From there, proceed to an X-intersection.
- Bear right onto the *Speedbag Trail*. Ignore one right fork and continue to an intersection with a dirt road.
- Bear right and pass remnants of the Alliance Mine. After a cement block building, bear left toward a utility station. Then quickly switchback to the right to follow a dirt road down to *Ontario Ridge Road*.
- Bear left onto this dirt road. Continue past a water tank to the left. Ignore a right fork and continue past mining history. Come to a left fork as the road bends right.
- Bear left onto *Ontario Ridge Trail*. Proceed straight past turn-offs. Arrive back on Prospect Avenue for the car. Descend the road and turn left onto Hillside Avenue for the trolley.

ROUTE SUMMARY:

o Start on the dirt trail at the top of Prospect Avenue.

o At a three-pronged fork, take the middle branch and come to a second fork. Proceed straight. Ignore a right fork. Come to an intersection with a dirt road.

o Turn left, then quickly turn right onto another dirt road and then immediately turn left onto the *Ontario Ridge Trail*. Come to a four-way intersection with the *TDS Ontario Bypass Trail* and proceed straight across it. Come to a three-way intersection.

o Bear right and quickly come to another intersection.

o Bear right onto the high side of *Empire Link Trail*. Ignore left forks. Continue to a wooden bridge. Cross a dirt road to continue on *Empire Link*. Proceed to an X-intersection.

o Bear right onto the *Speedbag Trail*. Ignore a right fork and follow the trail to an intersection with a dirt road.

o Bear right. After a cement block building, bear left and then quickly switchback right to descend to *Ontario Ridge Road*.

o Bear left. Follow this road to a left fork as the dirt road bends right.

o Bear left onto the *Ontario Ridge Trail*. Proceed straight back to start.

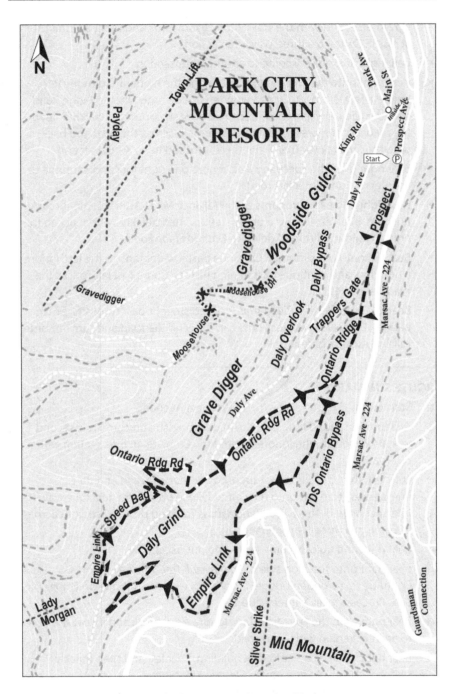

#14B Prospect - Empire Link

#15 Sweeney Switchbacks - 4:20

DESCRIPTION: This conveniently located hike on the Park City Mountain side of Old Town features some eye-popping architecture and an overview of how the town integrates with the ski resort.

Distance: 3.7 miles (6 km)
Elev. Gain: 887 feet (270 m)
Peak Elev: 7,929 feet (2,417 m)
Difficulty: *Difficult* though stairs and switchbacks help.
Configuration: Lollipop/figure eights.
Note: Not accessible in ski season.

DIRECTIONS:

- Ride the Main Street Trolley to the south end of Old Town or walk up Swede Alley from the Old Town Transit Center **bus stop**.

- **Drivers** may find parking in the two-tiered Sandridge parking lots west of Marsac Avenue at the south end of Old Town. In the upper parking lot, near the staircase between the two levels of parking, find a staircase down to Swede Alley.

- Opposite the south corner of Swede Alley, find an up staircase on the west side of Main Street. Ascend this staircase, cross Park Avenue and climb up another staircase to reach Woodside Avenue. Cross Woodside and ascend a third staircase to Norfolk Avenue.

- Turn right onto Norfolk and proceed to the end of the street where two trails begin. Take the *South Sweeney Trail* to the left, (though the sign says "North Sweeney"). Proceed through the switchbacks amidst private properties.

- Near a manhole cover at a fork with a curved arrow sign, make a sharp right turn.

- Come to another switchback at another manhole cover with a fork and make another sharp right turn. Continue across a rocky ski slope and come to a fork.

- Bear left. Proceed under the Town Chairlift. Come to a fork with a switchback.

- Bear left. Proceed through the switchbacks. Ignore a left fork and then ignore a right fork. Come to a switchback fork near a giant tree-filled hole.

- Bear left. Come to a four-way intersection with *Sweeney Trails* going both ways.

- Turn right going slightly uphill and quickly come to a four-way intersection.
- Turn left. Ignore a right footpath and come to a five-way intersection.
- Proceed straight and quickly come to a second right uphill trail marked *Johns*.
- Turn right onto *Johns Trail*. Come to a three-way intersection.
- Make a sharp left turn onto *4:20 Trail*. Ignore a right fork and arrive at a short, steep descent onto paved King Road. (If your shoe tread doesn't hold here, try going down backwards using toes and fingers.)
- Turn left onto King Road. You could follow it all the way back into town, but these directions take you to the *King Road Connect Trail*, which starts on the downhill side of the next big road curve.
- Turn left onto *King Road Connect*. Proceed straight as single-track becomes double-track. Come to a multi-trail intersection.
- Turn right and proceed downhill to a four-way intersection.
- Turn right onto *South Sweeney Trail*. Come to a fork with a left switchback.
- Proceed straight and come to a three-way intersection at a manhole cover.
- Proceed straight on this short trail back to King Road.
- Turn left onto King. Proceed past private driveways to an intersection with Sampson Avenue.
- Turn right on Sampson. Descend to the intersection with Norfolk Avenue. Directly across the street is the first of the three staircases that take you back to Main Street.
- Cross Main onto Swede Alley for the bus or the staircase back to Sandridge parking.

ROUTE SUMMARY:

o Find an up staircase on the west side of Main Street, opposite the south corner of Swede Alley. Climb three staircases to arrive on Norfolk Avenue.

o Turn right onto Norfolk and proceed to the end of the street. Take the trail to the left,

o At two switchbacks with forks, turn sharply right. Cross a rocky slope and come to a fork.

o Bear left. Come to a fork with a switchback.

o Bear left. Proceed through switchbacks, ignoring a left fork and then a right fork. Come to a switchback fork near a giant tree-filled hole.

o Bear left. Come to a four-way intersection.

o Turn right. Quickly come to a four-way intersection.

o Turn left. Ignore a right footpath and come to a five-way intersection.

o Proceed straight and quickly come to a second right uphill trail marked *Johns*.

o   Turn right onto *Johns*. Come to a three-way intersection.

o   Turn sharply left onto *4:20 Trail*. Ignore a right fork and arrive at a short, steep descent onto paved King Road.

o   Turn left onto King. On the downhill side of the next big road curve, find the start of the *King Road Connect Trail*.

o   Turn left onto this trail. Proceed to a multi-trail intersection.

o   Turn right and proceed downhill to a four-way intersection.

o   Turn right onto *South Sweeney*. Come to a fork with a left switchback.

o   Proceed straight and come to a three-way intersection at a manhole cover.

o   Proceed straight to King Road.

o   Turn left and proceed to the intersection with Sampson Avenue

o   Turn right on Sampson and descend to Norfolk Avenue. Directly across the street is a staircase that starts the downhill descent back to start.

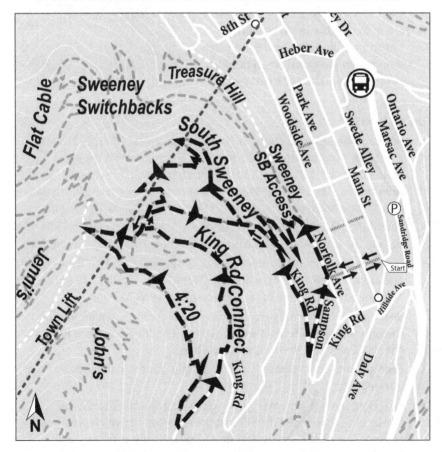

#15 Sweeney Switchbacks - 4:20

#16 Jenni's - Treasure Hill

DESCRIPTION: Jenni's Trail makes a big climb relatively easy. This popular route offers diverse landscapes and a broad sampling of the lower mountain terrain of Park City Resort.

Distance: 5 miles (8 km)

Elev. Gain: 885 feet (270 m)

Peak Elev: 7,802 feet (2,378 m)

Difficulty: *Intermediate.* Switchbacks help a lot.

Configuration: Loop.

Note: Not accessible in ski season.

◊ Restrooms, shopping, and dining are amongst the seasonal amenities of Park City Resort, as noted in Walk #1.

DIRECTIONS:

- Start at the southwest corner of the **parking** area at Park City Mountain, accessible from **bus stop** 1000, Park City Mountain. Walk between buildings with "The Lowell" and Legends Bar and Grill to your left. Bear right onto a plaza. Pass the Payday chairlift. Walk towards the Crescent chairlift and find a paved road ascending a ridge, *Jenni's Access Trail.*

- Turn right onto this paved path and at a fork with a dirt path, take the dirt path to the right. Atop the ridge come to *Jenni's Trail* going up and down.

- Turn left, heading uphill through trees. Cross under the First Time chairlift and cross a dirt road. Cross under the Three Kings chairlift twice and cross another dirt road. Come to an X-intersection with *CMG Trail.*

- Bear right onto *Jenni's Trail* continuing uphill through switchbacks under the Crescent chairlift. Cross a dirt road and continue under the Payday chairlift. Come to a three-way intersection.

- Bear left onto *Loose Moose Trail,* and quickly come to a five-way intersection.

- Bear right but not extreme right. You are now on *Flat Cable Trail* which borders the alpine slide thrill ride at the resort, so you might hear some screams. You might also be tempted to take the dirt road between switchbacks that winds down the ski slope. Don't, unless you want to risk slipping on loose gravel. *Flat Cable* leaves the slope and switchbacks into trees a few times. After seeing a sign with three ski slope names, wind through trees and come to a T-intersection with *Sweeney Switchbacks Trail*.

- Bear left, cross under the Town Chairlift and come to fork.
- Bear left onto *Treasure Hill Trail*. Ignore a right fork. Come to a fork at a switchback.
- Bear right. Cross a dirt road. Ignore a left fork and then ignore a right fork. Come to another fork.
- Bear left to continue on *Treasure Hill Trail* and cross a double-track. Ignore a left switchback and come to a dirt road.
- Turn left and the road becomes paved Lowell Avenue. Bear left. Lowell takes you back to the parking and bus stop at Park City Resort.

ROUTE SUMMARY:

o   At the plaza at the base of Park City Mountain Resort, pass the Payday chairlift, and find an uphill asphalt path before the Crescent chairlift.

o   Turn right onto this path. At a fork, bear right. Atop the ridge, turn left onto *Jenni's Trail*. Continue uphill under chairlifts, twice crossing dirt roads. Come to an X-intersection with *CMG Trail*.

o   Bear right onto *Jenni's Trail*. Cross a dirt road and come to a three-way intersection.

o   Bear left onto *Loose Moose Trail* and quickly come to a five-way intersection.

o   Bear right but not extreme right. Follow *Flat Cable Trail* to a T-intersection with *Sweeney Switchbacks Trail*.

o   Bear left and come to fork with *Treasure Hill Trail*.

o   Bear left onto *Treasure Hill*. Ignore a right fork and come to a fork at a switchback.

o   Bear right. Cross a dirt road. Ignore a left fork and a right fork and come to another fork.

o   Bear left to continue on *Treasure*. Cross a double-track. Ignore a left switchback and come to a dirt road.

o   Turn left and the dirt road becomes paved Lowell Avenue back to start.

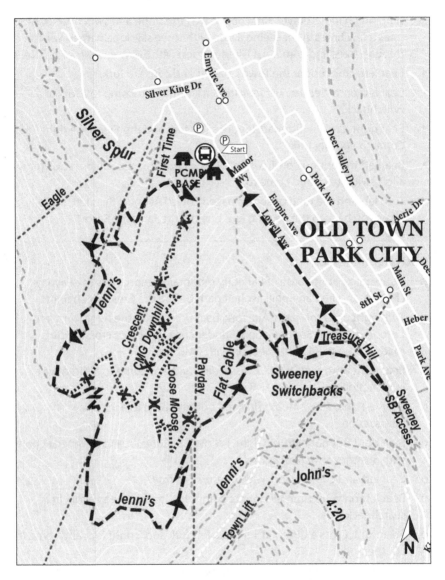

#16 Jenni's - Treasure Hill

#17 Armstrong - Dawns

DESCRIPTION: These beautiful trails are amongst the most popular for cyclists, hikers, and dog walkers. They are anchored by the amenities of the Silver Star and Park City Resorts.

Distance: 3.9 miles (6.3 km) or 4.5 miles (7.2 km)

Elev. Gain: 840 (256 m) or 811 feet (244 m)

Peak Elev: 7,668 feet (2,337 m)

Difficulty: *Intermediate.* It's steepest at the beginning. The shorter route climbs a bit more than the longer route.

Configuration: Lollipops.

Note: Not accessible in ski season.

◊ If you opt for Route B, see Hike #1 regarding the many amenities of Park City Mountain. The Route A starting point, Silver Star Resort, also offers shopping, dining and restrooms.

DIRECTIONS:

- For shorter **Route A** from Silver Star Resort, exit at the Silver Star North **bus stop.** Walk north to the elevator or walk up Silver Star Drive.
- Walk through the plaza and continue to a fork.
- Bear right onto the dirt road, *Silver Star Access* near the chairlift.
- For longer **Route B** from Park City Mountain, and for possible **parking**, exit at the PC Mountain **bus stop.** From the northwest corner of the north parking lot, find a dirt road to the right (north) of the First Time chairlift. Ascend this road. After the second chairlift tower, turn right onto a dirt path. It becomes Crescent Road. Come to a fork where the road bends right.
- Bear left. Just past the chairlift, make a left hairpin turn onto a dirt road, *Silver Star Access.*

- On *Silver Star Access* come to a fork. A sign shows the Armstrong Trail straight ahead. Ignore this sign and make a turn sharply right, also the *Armstrong Trail*, (with better views).
- Proceed under the chairlift on double-track to a fork.
- Bear right onto single-track and come to a fork.
- Bear right and proceed to a multi-trail intersection at the base of the King Con chairlift. Proceed straight to the far right of the chairlift and come to a fork.
- Bear left onto *Dawns Trail*. Proceed straight across a dirt road, under a chairlift and across ski slopes. Come to a fork.
- Bear left, continuing on *Dawns Trail*. Ignore some footpaths that deviate from the wider trail. At a fork, go either way to continue down *Dawns Trail* to a four-way intersection.
- For **Route A** and the bus, turn left and proceed back to the plaza and Three Kings Drive.
- For **Route B**, proceed across the double-track onto the single-track that veers right. Come to a four-way intersection.
- Proceed straight onto the *Silver Spur Trail*. It ends on a dirt road.
- Turn left to return to the resort base, parking and the bus.

ROUTE SUMMARY:

o For shorter **Route A** from Silver Star Resort, walk through the plaza and bear right onto the dirt road, *Silver Star Access*.

o For longer **Route B** from Park City Mountain, walk up the dirt road north of the First Time chairlift. Turn right onto a dirt path after the second chairlift tower. It becomes Crescent Road. Come to a fork and bear left.

o Just past the chair lift, make a hairpin turn to the left onto a dirt road, *Silver Star Access*.

o On *Silver Star Access* come to a fork. At a sign for the Armstrong Trail straight ahead, make a hairpin turn to the right.

o Proceed under the chairlift on double-track to a fork.

o Bear right onto single-track and come to a fork.

o Bear right and proceed to a multi-trail intersection at the base of the King Con chairlift.

o Proceed straight to the far right of the chairlift and come to a fork.

o Bear left onto *Dawns Trail*. Cross ski slopes and come to a fork.

o   Bear left, continuing on *Dawns Trail*. At a fork, go either way to continue down *Dawns* to a four-way intersection.

o   For **Route A** and the bus, turn left and proceed back to the Silver Star Resort.

o   For **Route B**, cross the double-track onto single-track. Come to a four-way intersection.

o   Proceed straight onto the *Silver Spur Trail*. It ends on a dirt road back to the resort base.

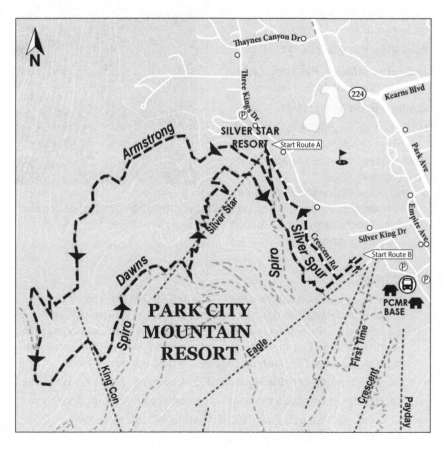

#17 Armstrong - Dawns

#18 Iron Mountain

DESCRIPTION: This challenging route offers stunning rock formations, shady firs and aspens, and a panoramic perspective on Park City's ski terrain. Even little rocks along these trails will paint your hike pink, coral, maroon and other shades of iron. Bigtooth maple trees bring brilliance to the lower terrain in autumn.

Distance: 7.8 miles (12.6 km), more for bus riders.

Elev. Gain: 1,942 feet (592 m), more by bus.

Peak Elev: 8,479 feet (2,584 m)

Difficulty: *Difficult.* Requires stamina and attentive footwork for miles.

Configuration: Long stem lollipop.

Note: Not accessible in ski season except for *Iron Mount Access* which by itself, makes for a good out-and-back hike with a lookout.

◊ It's possible that the trailhead for Iron Mt. Access might be relocated in the future. Trail closures or detours due to rockslides or construction might also occur here.

◊ Moose sightings are possible.

DIRECTIONS:

- Access from the nearest Meadows Drive and SR-224 **bus stop** is an arduous uphill walk for 0.9 mile (1.4 km), that adds 343 feet (105 m) elevation gain to an already strenuous hike. Very limited parking near the trailhead also adds some distance and elevation gain. Getting someone to drop you off at the trailhead may be the best way to get here.
- From the bus stop or if **driving,** from SR-224, turn west onto Meadows Drive.
- Take Meadows uphill to a three-way intersection with Aspen Springs Drive.
- Turn left onto Aspen Springs and proceed uphill to a three-way intersection with Delta Drive.
- Turn left onto Delta Drive and proceed to a three-way intersection with Iron Canyon Drive.
- Turn right onto Iron Canyon Drive and proceed to an intersection.
- Turn right onto Iron Mountain Drive and proceed around a bend. Pass a left turn and come to a right turn.

- Turn right onto Iron Canyon Court. Drivers might find parking on Iron Canyon Court or along Iron Mt. Drive. In the center of the cul-de-sac of Iron Canyon Court, find a trailhead.
- Start the climb on the hiking-only *Iron Mountain Access Trail*. Ignore multiple footpaths and deer trails to the left and right, starting almost as soon as you leave the trailhead. Stay on the main trail and after hiking uphill for about 1.2 miles, (2 km), notice a trail to the right, before a rocky ridge. There are several trails that will take you to a lookout bench on top of the ridge, and for some, just taking in the view from this lookout, and returning to the trailhead, is a good 3 mile (4.8 km) out-and-back hike. The **detour** to the ridge is recommended. The trail before and parallel to the rocky ridge has had a monster downed tree at its main entrance. You could climb over it or take a footpath below it.
- Turn right onto this trail (or turn left if coming down from the ridge) and follow it uphill until you come to an intersection with the *Mid Mountain Trail*.
- Turn right onto *Mid Mountain* and follow it through switchbacks, around a big bend and come to a fork.
- Turn left onto the *Ironman Trail*. Follow it across ski slopes and under the Iron Mountain Express chairlift. When the Quicksilver gondola comes into sight, *Iron Man Trail* will twice cross a dirt road. Continue to a fork with the *Goldfinger Trail*.
- Bear left and follow switchbacks down to a three-way intersection with *Mid Mountain Trail*.
- Turn right and quickly come to a fork.
- Bear left onto *Iron Mountain Access Trail*. Arrive at an intersection around the fallen tree.
- Bear left and descend back to paved Iron Canyon Court.
- Coming out of the cul-de-sac, turn left and then right onto Iron Canyon Drive. Come to a four-way intersection.
- Proceed straight and make the next left onto Delta Drive and come to an intersection.
- Turn right onto Aspen Springs Drive and come to a three-way intersection.
- Turn right onto Meadows Drive, which intersects SR-224 where there are ingoing and outgoing bus stops.

ROUTE SUMMARY:

o Find a trailhead in the center of the cul-de-sac in Iron Mountain Court and take the *Iron Mountain Access Trail* uphill for about 1.2 miles, (2 km). Find a trail to the right before a rocky ridge, with optional detour trails to a lookout on the ridge.

o Turn right onto this trail (or left if coming down from the ridge) and follow it uphill to an intersection with the *Mid Mountain Trail*.

o Turn right. Follow *Mid Mountain* to a fork.

o Turn left onto the *Iron Man Trail* and follow it across ski terrain. Twice cross a dirt road. Continue to a fork with the *Gold Finger Trail*.

o Bear left and follow switchbacks down to a three-way intersection with *Mid Mountain Trail*.

o Turn right and quickly come to a fork.

o Bear left onto the *Iron Mountain Access Trail* and arrive at an intersection near the fallen tree.

o Turn left and descend *Iron Mountain Access Trail* back to the trailhead.

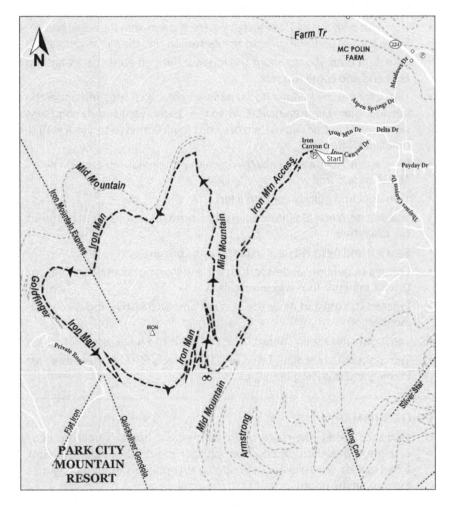

#18 Iron Mountain

#19 Masonic - Gambel Oak

DESCRIPTION: This easily accessed hike on the east side of Park City provides prime panoramas of Old Town and its suburbs, ski resorts, golf courses, the Deer Valley duck ponds, and the surrounding mountains.

Distance: 4.2 miles (6.8 km)

Elev. Gain: 577 feet (176 m)

Peak Elev: 7,546 feet (2,307 m)

Difficulty: *Intermediate.* Climbs are short and interspersed with level ground.

Configuration: Loop.

DIRECTIONS:

- From Park Avenue at Town Lift **bus stop**, walk north on Park Avenue to the intersection with 9th Street. (There could be a bus stop on Main St. and 9th St.)
- Turn right on Ninth and follow it as circles around to Main Street. Continue east on Main Street to Deer Valley Drive.
- If **driving**, turn east off of Deer Valley Drive onto Aerie Drive and find very limited parking to the right. If unavailable, park in Old Town and walk back.
- On the north side of Aerie Drive, find the *Lost Prospector Trail*, below the parking area. (The south side of *Lost Prospector Trail* is above the parking.)
- Take the trail on the north side of Aerie Drive and soon come to a four-way X-intersection.
- Turn to the extreme right onto the *Masonic Trail* and follow it to another X-intersection.
- Bear left here, but not extreme left. Continue to a three-way intersection.
- Turn left and proceed to a fork.
- Bear right and continue on the *Masonic Trail* to an intersection.
- Proceed straight. Continue past a power line road to another four-way intersection.
- Proceed straight in the direction of the *Gambel Oak Trail* to another four-way intersection.

- Proceed straight again and the trail ends on paved Mellow Mountain Road.
- Turn right onto the road and proceed uphill to a curve. At the center of the road curve find a trail on the left.
- Turn left onto this trail and quickly come to a fork.
- Bear left onto the *Lost Prospector Trail* and continue to a four-way intersection.
- Turn left, but not extreme left, and come to a power line crossing.
- Turn left under the power line and quickly turn right back onto the trail. Continue until you come to the paved road you started on, Aerie Drive.
- Turn left on Aerie to return to parking, or to Deer Valley Drive and Old Town.

ROUTE SUMMARY:

o Start at the *Lost Prospector Trail* on the north side of Aerie Drive. Come to a four-way intersection.

o Turn sharply right onto *Masonic Trail* and follow it to another X-intersection.

o Bear left, but not extreme left. Continue to a three-way intersection.

o Turn left and proceed to a fork.

o Bear right and continue on *Masonic Trail* to a four-way intersection.

o Proceed straight. Continue past a power line road to another four-way intersection.

o Proceed straight to the *Gambel Oak Trail* and arrive at another four-way intersection.

o Proceed straight again. The trail ends on Mellow Mountain Road.

o Turn right onto the paved road and proceed uphill to a curve. Find a trail to the left.

o Turn left onto this trail and quickly come to a fork.

o Bear left onto *Lost Prospector Trail* and continue to a four-way intersection.

o Turn left, but not extreme left, and come to a power line crossing.

o Turn left under the power line and quickly turn right back onto the trail. Continue until you come to Aerie Drive to return to start.

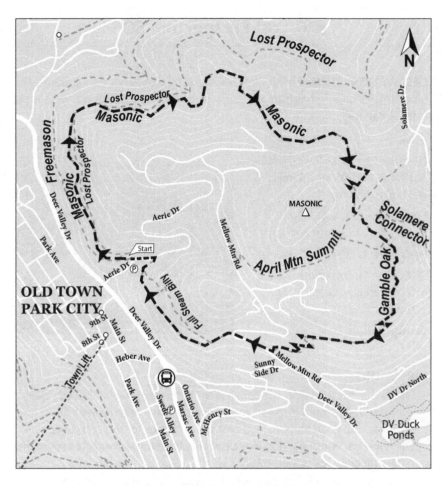

#19 Masonic - Gamble Oak

#20 Lost Prospector - SOS

DESCRIPTION: Starting in the Iron Horse district of Park City's suburbs, this hike features panoramas from the north side of Masonic Hill and traverses the historic Rail Trail.

Distance: 3.7 miles (6 km) but bus riders can add about 1.5 miles (2.4 km) round trip.

Elev. Gain: 700 feet (213 m). A little more from the bus stop.

Peak Elev: 7,230 feet (2,204 m)

Difficulty: *Intermediate,* due to a moderately steep climb at the start.

Configuration: Loop.

DIRECTIONS:

- Ride the bus to the closest Bonanza Drive **bus stop** available. Bus riders and **drivers** should turn east from Bonanza Drive onto Lower Iron Horse Loop Road and proceed past the buildings to the road curve near dumpsters. Visitor parking may be available near the dumpsters, or in the parking lot in spots marked "V."
- From the east end of Iron Horse Loop Road, walk uphill. Find concrete steps at the east end of the upper most buildings and a footpath, the *Hang Time South Trail,* left of the steps.
- Bear left onto the footpath and climb for about 0.4 miles (0.6 km), after which this route becomes easy. Arrive at an intersection with the *Freemason Trail.*
- Continue straight and arrive at another intersection with the *Lost Prospector Trail.*
- Turn left (though the *Lost Prospector Trail* also goes right). Proceed on this trail ignoring a left turn. Continue straight across a double-track road and quickly come to a fork.
- Bear left and continue to a five-way intersection.

- Bear left in the direction of the *Gambel Oak North Trail,* and then ignore a left turn to this same trail. Proceed through two switchbacks and ignore a left turn at the next switchback. About 2.3 miles (3.7 km) from start, arrive at a left intersecting single-track, the *SOS Trail.*

- Turn left and immediately turn left again onto *SOS.* Descend on multiple short switchbacks. Ignore a right turn, and ignore the straight path between this trail's loops made by naughty cyclists. Unless you don't mind scratched ankles, the recommended route is to stay on the wider trail and descend on the switchbacks, ignoring a left footpath turn off.

- When you come to a fork, bear left and quickly come to a dirt road.

- Turn left onto this road and bear right at a fork that comes up just before condos. This brings you to the pavement of the *Rail Trail.*

- Turn left onto the *Rail Trail* and proceed until you've gone about 3.3 miles (5.3 km) from start. Come upon a footpath to the left, opposite a blacktop trail to the right.

- Turn left onto this footpath and after a short ascent turn right. You will now be walking parallel to the *Rail Trail* on the *Bonanza Trail.* Arrive at an X-intersection.

- Bear right and continue on the ridgeline trail, ignoring some right turns back to the *Rail Trail.* Come to a trail intersection with the *Freemason Trail.*

- Proceed straight and the trail will turn into double-track and then into a short uphill single-track. It quickly brings you back to the dumpster and parking along Iron Horse Loop Road.

- Descend to Bonanza Drive and turn right for the bus stop.

ROUTE SUMMARY:

o   From the east end of Iron Horse Loop Road, proceed uphill to a footpath left of buildings.

o   Ascend on this footpath to an intersection with the *Freemason Trail.*

o   Continue straight and arrive at another intersection with *Lost Prospector Trail.*

o   Turn left. Ignore a left turn and continue straight across a double-track road to a fork.

o   Bear left and proceed to a five-way intersection.

o   Bear left towards *Gambel Oak North Trail* and then ignore a left turn to this same trail. Proceed through two switchbacks and ignore a left turn at the next switchback. After about 2.3 miles (3.7 km) from start, arrive at a left intersecting single-track, the *SOS Trail.*

o   Turn left and immediately turn left again. Descend on short switchbacks. Ignore a left footpath turn off.

o   When you come to a fork, bear left and proceed to a dirt road.

o   Turn left onto the road and come to a fork before condos.

o   Bear right and arrive at the paved *Rail Trail*.

o   Turn left and proceed until you've gone about 3.3 miles (5.3 km) from start. Arrive at a footpath to the left, opposite a blacktop trail to the right.

o   Turn left onto this footpath and then quickly turn right onto single-track. Proceed to an X-intersection.

o   Bear right and continue on the ridgeline trail to a trail intersection.

o   Proceed straight and arrive back at Iron Horse Loop Road.

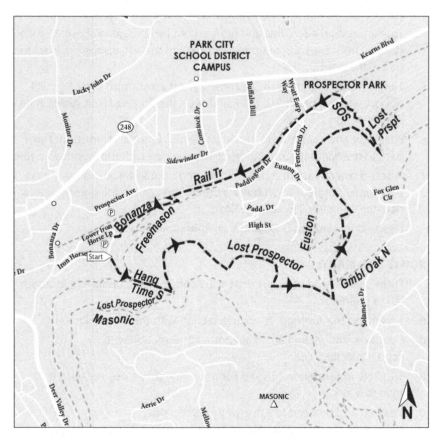

#20 Lost Prospector - SOS

#21 Skid Row - Euston

DESCRIPTION: The playgrounds of Prospector Park, the wetlands of Silver Creek, shady slopes on Masonic Hill, ridgeline lookouts, and exquisite estates in Solamere, are all settings for this hike from the Union Pacific Historic Rail Trail in Prospector, to the upper reaches of residential Deer Valley.

Distance: 4.4 miles (7.1 km), more for bus riders.

Elev. Gain: 584 feet (178 m)

Peak Elev: 7,238 feet (2,206 m)

Difficulty: *Intermediate.* There's a long gentle climb to start.

Configuration: Loop.

DIRECTIONS:

- The bus stop at Wyatt Earp Way takes you to Prospector Park directly, or the Comstock Drive **bus stop** provides alternative access and adds about a mile (1.6 km) round-trip distance to this route. From the Comstock bus stop, walk north on Comstock to the paved *Kearns Bike Path (a.k.a. Park City Parkway)*, just before the traffic light on SR-248.
- Turn right onto this paved path and proceed past a second road intersection at Wyatt Earp Way. The bike path turns right into Prospector Park here.
- **Drivers** may find limited parking in Prospector Park by turning south off of SR-248 onto Wyatt Earp Way, just SW of PC Hill. Then immediately turn left into the park.
- From Prospector Park, follow the paved path east. It merges with the *Rail Trail.*
- Turn left onto the paved *Rail Trail* and proceed east for about 0.7 miles (1.1 km), passing houses, the *SOS Trail,* and maybe beaver lodges. Come to a dirt road forking right.
- Bear right onto this road and immediately come to an intersection with another dirt road and the *Skid Row Trail.*
- Bear left onto *Skid Row* and continue through multiple switchbacks to arrive at an intersection with the *Lost Prospector Trail.*
- Bear left to continue on *Skid Row* through more switchbacks, and come to a four-way intersection with the *Fox Tail Trail.*

- Turn sharply right onto *Fox Tail*, and follow it uphill to the top of the ridge. This trail offers some grand views before intersecting with a paved road, Fox Glen Circle.
- Cross the road and follow the circular path on the left to a second paved road.
- Turn left on this road and come to an intersection with Solamere Drive.
- Turn right onto Solamere. Ascend for a short distance and come upon a sign on the right for *Gambel Oak Park North*, marking a dirt road.
- Turn right onto this double-track and proceed downhill under power lines until you come to a trail and a sign reading *"Trail."*
- Turn right onto the single-track diverging away from the power lines, and continue on this trail to a three-way intersection with the *Lost Prospector Trail*.
- Turn right and immediately come to a fork.
- Bear left onto *Gambel Oak North Trail* and follow it to a dirt road, the *Euston Trail*.
- Turn right and follow the dirt road to paved Euston Drive. Continue downhill on Euston until it ends on Paddington Drive. Look for a footpath on the opposite side of paved Paddington. Take this footpath just a few steps back to the paved *Rail Trail*.
- Bus riders should turn right for the Wyatt Earp Way bus stop or left for the Comstock bus stop, depending on which is serviced. For the Comstock bus stop, turn left onto the *Rail Trail* and proceed west to an intersecting trail on the right, the *Kearns Bike Path*.
- Turn right onto *Kearns* and follow it through a parking lot to Sidewinder Drive.
- Cross Sidewinder and continue north on the sidewalk along Comstock Drive until you come to the starting bus stop.
- Drivers should turn right onto the *Rail Trail* and proceed to the first road intersection with Wyatt Earp Way.
- Turn left onto Wyatt Earp and find Prospector Park parking on the right.

ROUTE SUMMARY:

o Start on the paved path in Prospector Park on Wyatt Earp Way.

o Follow the path from the park eastward and merge with the *Rail Trail*, bearing left.

o Proceed to a dirt road forking right.

o Bear right and immediately come to an intersection.

o Turn left onto *Skid Row Trail* and continue to an intersection with *Lost Prospector Trail*.

o Bear left and continue on *Skid Row* to a four-way intersection with *Fox Tail Trail*.

o Turn sharply right onto *Fox Tail* and follow it to a paved road.

o   Cross the road and follow the circular path on the left to another road.

o   Turn left on this paved road and arrive at an intersection.

o   Turn right. Proceed uphill to a sign on the right to *Gambel Oak Park North.*

o   Turn right onto this double-track and proceed downhill to a sign marked "*Trail.*"

o   Turn right onto single-track and continue to a three-way intersection with *Lost Prospector Trail.*

o   Turn right and immediately come to a fork.

o   Bear left onto *Gambel Oak North Trail* and follow it to a dirt road.

o   Turn right and follow the road to paved Euston Drive until it ends on Paddington Drive.

o   Cross Paddington to find a footpath back to the *Rail Trail.*

o   Bus riders have two possible stops as noted in the directions above.

o   Drivers turn right onto the *Rail Trail.* Proceed to Wyatt Earp Way.

o   Turn left onto Wyatt Earp. Prospector Park parking is on the right.

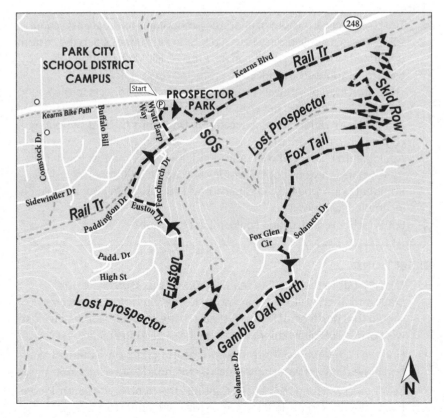

#21 Skid Row - Euston

#22 PC Hill

DESCRIPTION: Trails to the top of this monogrammed hill provide a good climb with outstanding views of the mountains, resorts, the school campus, and the links and lakes of Park Meadows.

Distance: 3.3 miles (5.2 km) more by bus.

Elev. Gain: 536 feet (163 m)

Peak Elev: 7,170 feet (2,185 m)

Difficulty: *Intermediate*, starting with a moderately steep climb.

Configuration: Loop.

Note:

◊ The controversial custom of imprinting mountains to broadcast school spirit is seen mostly in the western U.S. Some historians claim the custom originated to help orient railroaders. Atop PC Hill, a dedication rock honors contributors to Park City's protected open space.

◊ The return loop of this walk provides some shade, connects to the Round Valley trail system, and traverses a neighborhood of mountain mansions and wetlands within the school campus. Don't miss the bird symphony coming from the "sanctuary."

◊ Apologies to readers who already found this route amongst the thirty routes in my previous book, *Park City Walking Guide*. It's the only route from that book repeated here, because a Park City hiking book would be incomplete without it.

◊ Future school construction could impact this route.

DIRECTIONS:

▪ Take the bus to the Park City Learning Center **bus stop** on Kearns Boulevard. Then walk east along north Kearns. Bus riders and **drivers** should turn north off of Kearns just east of the school buildings, and just west of PC Hill. Follow this road to a trailhead parking area.

▪ Find the *PC Hill Trail* opposite a footbridge. Turn right onto this trail to begin the climb and ascend through a switchback. Arrive at a fork.

▪ Bear right, switching back again. Continue the climb going south. Ignore two fooler trails to the left and one to the right. Come to a fork.

▪ Bear left and the trail bends east. Stay on the path that appears most used.

- Notice a left turn as a fence comes into view ahead. There's a trail to the left before the fence, and another trail along the fence. Turn left onto either and proceed through the next left turn onto a trail that doubles back west and takes you to the "PC" letters.
- Turn right onto either of the trails above the big "P" or "C." Both go a short distance to the mountaintop where there are more trails, including *PC Hill Trail* to the east.
- Take the *PC Hill Trail* downhill through switchbacks. Cross a double-track dirt road and stay on the single-track. Come to a fork marked "Quinn Recreation Trails."
- Bear left, and quickly come to a trail intersection with the *Hat Trick Trail*.
- Turn left onto *Hat Trick* and continue to the next intersection with the *Fairway Hills Connector Trail*.
- Turn left onto *Fairway Hills Connector*. It ends in the cul-de-sac of Morning Sky Court. Continue downhill on Morning Sky to its end on Silver Cloud Drive.
- Turn left onto Silver Cloud and follow it downhill to Meadows Drive.
- Turn left onto Meadows Drive and cautiously walk in the bike lane. Just past a private drive on the left, (that looks like a road), find a blacktop path that goes back to the school fields, and a sign pointing to the *Rail Trail*.
- Turn left onto this path and bear right onto a woodchip trail bordering a fence that goes around the school athletic field. This trail takes you past the bird "sanctuary" south of the field, and comes to a footbridge that goes back to trailhead parking at the base of PC Hill.
- From the trailhead, exit south to Kearns Boulevard. To get to the **bus,** turn right onto Kearns Boulevard and walk west.

ROUTE SUMMARY:

o   Start at the PC Trailhead, east of the public-school campus and west of PC Hill.

o   Turn right onto the *PC Hill Trail* and begin the climb.

o   Proceed through two switchbacks. Bear right at an intersection. Ignore some fooler trails and come to a fork.

o   Bear left. Notice two left turns before a fence.

o   Take either left and proceed as these trails turn left and bend west to arrive at "PC."

o   Take either of the trails that start above the big "P" or "C" to the top of the mountain.

o   Take the *PC Hill Trail* on the east side of the mountaintop. At an intersection with double-track, cross the road to stay on the single-track. Arrive at a fork.

o   Bear left at this fork and quickly arrive at the *Hat Trick Trail*.

o   Turn left onto *Hat Trick* and come to an intersection.

o   Turn left onto *Fairway Hills Connector Trail* and proceed to paved Morning Sky Court that takes you downhill onto Silver Cloud Drive and ends on Meadows Drive.

o   Turn left onto Meadows. Come to a blacktop path on the left entering the school grounds.

o   Turn left onto the blacktop and then bear right onto a woodchip path encircling the athletic field to arrive at a footbridge that returns to start.

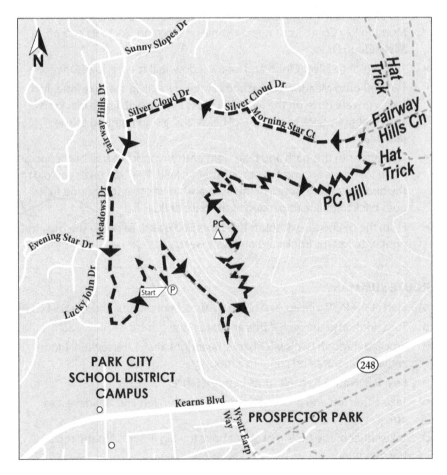

#22 PC Hill

#23 Quarry Mountain

DESCRIPTION: A hiking-only trail on Quarry Mountain offers exceptional views and an amazing array of spring flowers; but you'll need this guidebook for tricky navigation.

Distance: 3.2 miles (5.2 km)

Elev. Gain: 685 feet (209 m)

Peak Elev: 7,371 feet (2,247 m)

Difficulty: *Difficult* due to a long steady climb.

Configuration: Loop.

Note: Easily combined with Hike #24, McPolin Farm Nature Trail.

DIRECTIONS:

- Ride the **bus** or **drive** to the Farm Trailhead on the east side of SR-224, across the highway from the white barn. Proceed south on a paved path to a narrow stone staircase south of the parking, and ascend on the *Quarry Mountain Trail* to a T-intersection.
- Turn left and wind up the mountain, ignoring deer trails along the way. At two definitive intersections, turn left. At a third intersection turn right. (The left fork goes to a lookout bench, worth the **detour**.) Continue to a utility station on the mountaintop.
- Proceed past the fence to find a narrow trail after its northeast corner. Take this trail downhill through nine switchbacks. Bear right at two forks. The trail goes uphill a short way and ends at a T-intersection.
- Turn left and continue downhill. Bear right at the first intersection and left at the next intersection. The trail ends on the paved cul-de-sac of Mountain Ridge Court.
- Walk north onto the street, passing two houses and a rock wall. When you come to the next house, look for a single-track at the corner of the home's driveway.
- Turn right onto this trail. Tight vegetation gives way to a red clay ridgeline trail overlooking wetlands, which brings you back to the Farm Trailhead, parking and bus stop.

ROUTE SUMMARY:

o   Start at the Farm Trailhead east of SR-224, opposite the white barn. Proceed south to stone steps at the end of the parking and follow the trail to a T-intersection.

o   Turn left. Continue uphill, turning left at two intersections and right at a third intersection.

o   On the mountaintop, proceed around a utility fence to find a narrow trail at its northeast corner. Follow this trail downhill, bearing right at two forks. Arrive at a T-intersection.

o   Turn left and follow the trail to another intersection.

o   Turn right and continue to another intersection.

o   Turn left and continue downhill to a paved cul-de-sac. On this street, find a single-track at the corner of a driveway on your right.

o   Turn right onto this narrow trail and follow it back to start.

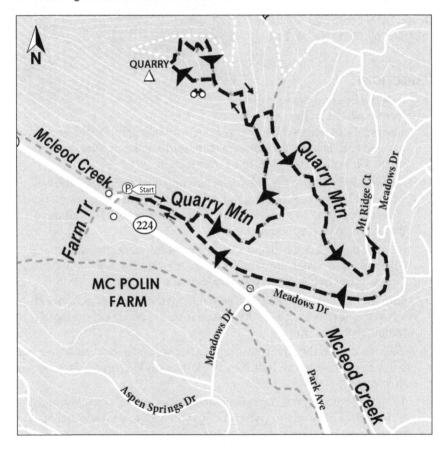

#23 Quarry Mountain

#24 McPolin Farm Nature Trail

DESCRIPTION: Paved trails along this easy route take you through Park City's entry corridor and the iconic McPolin farm. The farm and the Nature Trail feature plaques that provide education about local history and environment phenomena.

Distance: 1.7 miles (2.7 km)

Elev. Gain: 195 feet (59 m)

Peak Elev: 6,863 feet (2,092 m)

Difficulty: *Easy*, the easiest in this guidebook.

Configuration: Lollipop.

Note: Not accessible in cross-country ski season.

◊ The historic McPolin Barn and vintage farm equipment are part of an 80-acre compound that helped to feed Park City's early settlers. Park City Municipal purchased this property in 1990 as preserved open space. Restrooms are available in the back of the building northwest of the barn.

◊ The *Farm Trail* traditionally features a scarecrow contest in autumn.

◊ This route is easily combined with Hike #23 Quarry Mountain.

DIRECTIONS:

▪ Ride to either of the McPolin Farm **bus stops** on the east or west sides of SR-224. **Drivers** may find trailhead parking on the east side of SR-224 across the highway from the white barn.

▪ Turn north out of the parking area, or south from the east bus stop, onto paved paths that lead to a signpost that points to the *Farm Trail* and a tunnel to the west side of SR-224.

▪ Cross under the highway and turn right coming out of the underpass. Then turn left onto either of two paved paths through the farm. Both paths lead to another asphalt path at the farm's southwest end.

▪ Turn right onto the paved *Farm Trail* behind the farm, and proceed a short distance to a plaque on the left that marks the start of the hiking-only *McPolin Nature Trail*.

- Turn left onto this single-track and follow it to its north intersection with the *Farm Trail*.

- Turn right and return to the farm where you can explore some more. Turn east onto any of the paths that pass through the farm going to the bus stop on west SR-224, or the paved trail that turns right to go under the highway, back to parking or the eastside bus stop.

ROUTE SUMMARY:

o Take the bus to either of the McPolin Farm bus stops, or park at the Farm Trailhead on the east side of SR-224.

o From the east side of 224, take the tunnel under the highway and follow a paved path that bends right and turns left into the farm. Proceed through the farm to arrive at another paved path behind the farm.

o Turn right and proceed a short distance to the hiking-only *McPolin Nature Trail* on the left.

o Turn left onto this trail and follow it back to its intersection with the paved *Farm Trail*.

o Turn right and return to the farm and bus stop on the west side of the highway, or proceed under the highway through the tunnel to the east bus stop or parking.

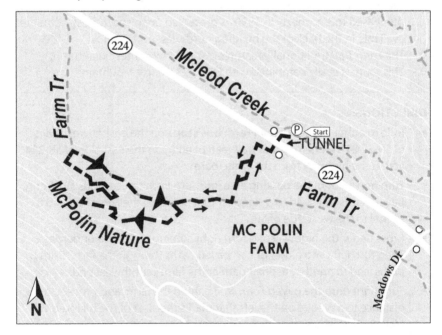

#24 McPolin Farm Nature Trail

#25 Holly's

DESCRIPTION: Occasionally edgy, this hike traverses fifteen of Park City Mountain's northern ski slopes and takes you through some of the amenities of the Canyons Village. Start out in sunshine but most of this route rambles through shady forest.

Distance: 4.8 miles (7.7 km) from the top of the cabriolet.

Elev. Gain: 953 feet (290 m)

Peak Elev: 7,737 feet (2,358 m)

Difficulty: *Difficult* Though switchbacks help, you'll climb for most of the first two miles (3.2 km). Be extra cautious about cyclists at intersections and where the trail rims steep embankments.

Configuration: Long stem lollipop.

Note:
◊ Resort offerings include dining, gondola rides, an 18-hole golf course, alpine disc golf, miniature golf, a bike park, zip line tours, horseback riding, mountain lake fishing, pedal boats, and lift assisted mountain biking and hiking in summer. Information is available at *parkcitymountain.com*.
◊ The cabriolet is an aerial transport system that takes people from the bus stop and parking area along the west side of SR-224, to the base of the ski area in the Canyons Village. There's no cost to ride, but it operates only during peak times.

DIRECTIONS:
▪ Take the bus to the Grand Summit Hotel **bus stop** and walk uphill to the Canyons Village plaza. If the cabriolet is running, you can take a city bus to the Canyons Resort Transit Hub and take the cabriolet to the resort plaza. **Drivers** turn west from SR-224 onto Canyons Resort Drive and following around 3/4 of the traffic circle to the parking lot at the base of the cabriolet. When the cabriolet is not running, drivers can take a bus or walk up to base of the resort.

- From the top of the cabriolet, facing the gondola, turn right and walk past the mini golf course towards the Orange Bubble Express chairlift. There's a dirt road before the chairlift.

- Turn left onto the dirt road and walk uphill. Pass a dirt road to the left and find a single-track trailhead on the left, just where a building begins on the far right. This is *Holly's Trail*.

- Turn left onto *Holly's* and follow it uphill to the switchbacks between the bubble chairlift and the gondola. Do not take shortcuts between the switchbacks, as there's a possibility of winding up on the *Richochet Trail*, the switchbacks of which parallel *Holly's Trail* but are for downhill cyclists only. *Holly's* switchbacks keep crossing a dirt road and after the seventh switchback on this ski slope, the trail appears to end on the dirt road.

- Turn right, walk a few paces uphill, and pick up the single-track trail again on the right. Follow it through more switchbacks and it will veer into trees to the right. The trail now becomes a straight shot along a ridge overlooking the golf course. Continue until the trail comes downhill to a dirt road.

- Cross the road and follow the single-track trail uphill on the other side. Ignore a left turn and come to an overgrown dirt road tracking down a ski slope.

- Cross the dirt road and continue on the single-track. The trail will again bend down to a dirt road. Ignore an overgrown dirt road ascending a ski slope to the left and just after, turn left onto a red dirt road. For about 0.3 mi (0.5 km) you'll climb, but only the first 0.1mile (0.2 km) is steep. Pass a building uphill to the left and shortly after; find a single-track trail on the right. This is *Holly's Trail* again.

- Turn right onto *Holly's* and follow it across a ski slope road to a three-way intersection.

- Turn right to stay on *Holly's*. Continue across the ski slope road again, and the trail again drops down to a dirt road.

- Cross the road and bear left onto the single-track. Proceed to an intersection with a dirt road.

- Cross the road and bear left, and the trail takes you back to the ski slope at the base of the resort. You now have two options. The recommended option is to follow the switchbacks back to the dirt road next to the Orange Bubble Express chairlift to return to the plaza and cabriolet. Or, at the risk of slipping and sliding, you could walk straight down the dirt road to the resort plaza.

ROUTE SUMMARY:

o From the top of the cabriolet in the Canyons Village, turn right towards the Orange Bubble Express chairlift. There's a dirt road just before the bubble chair.

o Turn left onto this road and walk uphill. Find a single-track trailhead on the left, after a dirt road to the left, and opposite where a building starts on the far right.

o Turn left onto this single-track, and follow it through switchbacks. After the seventh switchback, turn right onto the dirt road, and quickly pick up the single-track again on the right, a few paces uphill. Follow it through more switchbacks and into trees. Continue to a dirt road.

o Cross the road and follow the single-track trail uphill. The trail will bend down to a red dirt road.

o Turn left onto this dirt road and continue uphill for about 0.3 mi (0.5 km). Find a single-track trail on the right

o Turn right and follow the single-track to a three-way intersection.

o Turn right to stay on *Holly's Trail*. Continue until the trail again drops to a dirt road.

o Cross the road and bear left onto single-track. Proceed to another intersection with a dirt road.

o Cross the road and bear left. *Holly's Trail* now takes you back to the switchbacks and the Canyons Village Plaza.

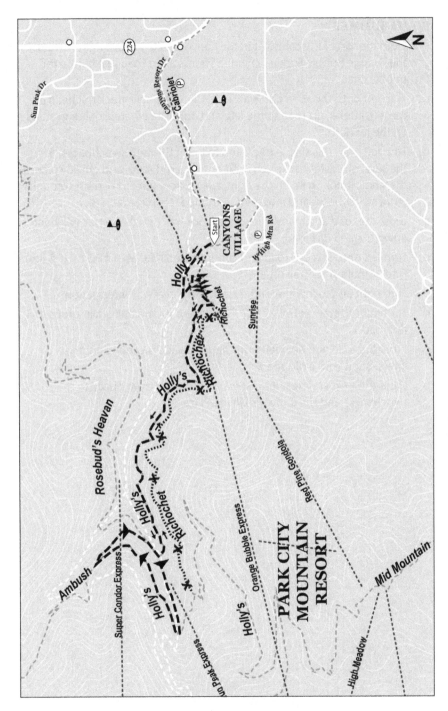

#25 Holly's

#26 Dubois - Collins

DESCRIPTION: These neighborhood trails take you through wetlands and mature shady forests. This route is one of the prettiest and most easily navigated in the entire trail system.

Distance: 3.1 miles (5 km)

Elev. Gain: 650 feet (198 m)

Peak Elev. 6,683 feet (2,037 m)

Difficulty: *Intermediate* There's a gentle but steady climb for about 1.5 miles (2.5 km)

Configuration: Loop.

DIRECTIONS:

- Ride to the Park City Nursery **bus stop** at the southwest intersection of Bear Hollow Drive and SR-224. Walk west along Bear Hollow to the Sun Peak Clubhouse parking on the right, about 0.2 mi (0.3 km). **Drivers** may find parking in the lot of the Park City Community Church on the south side of Bear Hollow Drive, across the street from the Sun Peak Clubhouse. However, church parking is closed to trail users on Sundays until noon.
- Find the *Dubois Trail* at the NE end of the Sun Peak clubhouse (private) parking area.
- Turn right onto the *Dubois Trail* and follow it as it winds through the neighborhood with occasional road crossings. Ignore intersecting footpaths to private residences. Ignore the *Enclave Trail* intersection to the right. *Dubois Trail* switchbacks up a ridge and ends after two posts onto the *Collins Trail*.
- Turn left onto *Collins* and follow it through switchbacks downhill. Ignore an intersecting trail to the left and arrive on paved Sun Peak Drive.
- Turn left and come to the corner of Bear Hollow Drive.
- Turn right and descend back to the bus stop or church parking.

ROUTE SUMMARY:

o   Start at the trailhead at the east end of the Sun Peak Clubhouse private parking lot

o   Turn right onto the *Dubois Trail* and follow uphill for about 1.5 miles (2.5 km). Ignore intersecting trails, and come to a three-way intersection with the *Collins Trail.*

o   Turn left onto Collins and follow it downhill. Ignore an intersecting trail to the left, and arrive on paved Sun Peak Drive.

o   Turn left and come to the corner of Bear Hollow Drive.

o   Turn right to return to start.

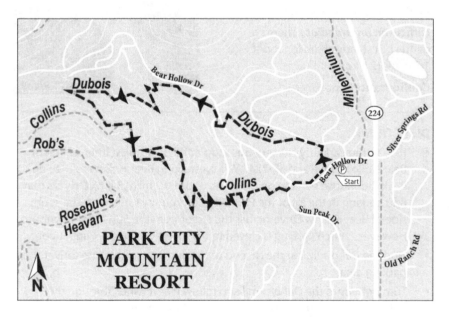

#26 Dubois - Collins

#27 Rob's - Rosebud's Heaven

DESCRIPTION: Enjoy deep forest, fields of flowers and fantastic views of the ski trails and canyons of the north side of Park City Mountain Resort.

Distance: 7.2 miles (11.5 km)

Elev. Gain: 1,560 feet (476 m)

Peak Elev: 7,874 feet (2,400 m)

Difficulty: *Difficult*. There are two gentle but long climbs.

Configuration: Lollipop.

Note: Not accessible in ski season.

◊ *Ambush Trail* can be hot and dusty. Reversing the direction of this loop is a cooler option for late starters, but the climbs are a little more challenging. Some benches offer rest.

◊ Avoid this hike if high winds. There are many dead trees along shady *Rob's Trail*.

◊ Hike #25 Holly's or #26 Dubois - Collins, offer additional access options for hikers looking for an even longer hiking experience.

DIRECTIONS:

▪ Getting here by **bus** is challenging. The Park City Nursery bus stop on SR-224 is about 1.5 miles (2.4 km) from the trailhead and it's a steep climb for walkers up Bear Hollow Drive. You can also get to the trailhead by taking a free Olympic Park bus to the top of the park. Inquire about park bus service in the Visitor Information Center on the corner of SR-224 and Olympic Parkway. If bus service is available, ride to the top of Olympic Park and pass around the gait onto Bear Hollow Drive. Then walk downhill about 0.8 miles (1.3 km). Note a trailhead with parking to the right. Now you just need a plan to get back uphill to the Olympic Park, or walk downhill on Bear Hollow Road 1.5 miles (2.4 km). You can also access the *Rob's* Trailhead from the Iron Bill Trail noted in hike #29 Olympic Park Loop, or hike to it from Holly's Trail, #25, or from the Collins Trail in hike #26. Another option is to have someone drop you off and pick you up.

▪ **Drivers** should turn west from SR-224 onto Bear Hollow Drive and proceed uphill 1.5 miles (2.4 km) to limited parking on the left.

- Begin at the trailhead on *Rob's Trail* and proceed to a fork with the *Collins Trail*.
- Bear right and continue on *Rob's Trail* to another fork with the *Rosebud's Heaven Trail*.
- Bear right and proceed uphill on *Rob's Trail* to an intersection with *Ambush* and *Olympic Trails*.
- Bear left onto the *Ambush Trail* and proceed to a dirt road. Cross the road to the trail on the other side and come to a fork with *Holly's Trail* going both ways.
- Bear left onto *Holly's Trail* going downhill to another fork.
- Bear left and again cross the dirt road to pick up the *Rosebud's Heaven Trail* on the other side. This trail ascends the ridge with switchbacks, circles around the ridge, and comes to a fork with *Rob's Trail* going both ways.
- Bear right onto *Rob's Trail* going downhill.
- At the next fork with the *Collins Trail*, bear left towards *Rob's Trail,* and arrive back at the trailhead on Bear Hollow Road.

ROUTE SUMMARY:

o   Begin on *Rob's Trail* at the Bear Hollow Road Trailhead.

o   Bear right at the first fork, continuing on *Rob's Trail*. Come to another fork.

o   Bear right and continue on *Rob's Trail* uphill to an intersection.

o   Bear left onto *Ambush Trail*, crossing a dirt road. Continue to a fork with *Holly's Trail*.

o   Bear left onto *Holly's Trail* going downhill to another fork.

o   Bear left, cross the dirt road, and follow *Rosebud's Heaven* up and around the ridge to a fork.

o   Bear right onto *Rob's Trail* going downhill to another fork.

o   Bear left to *Rob's Trail* to return to start.

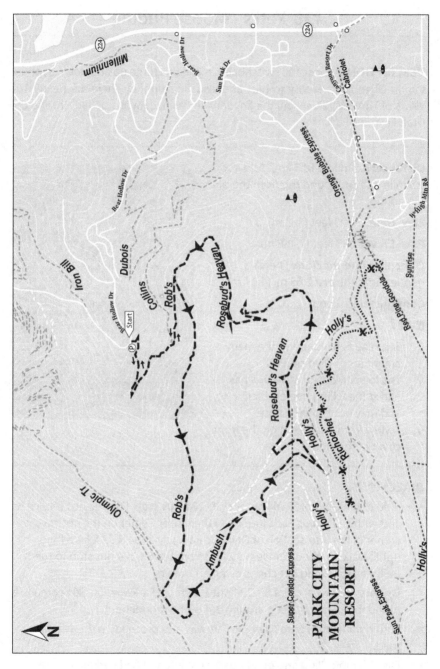

#27 Rob's - Rosebud's Heaven

#28 Yeti's - Moose Puddle

DESCRIPTION: Almost 100 switchbacks make this route up and down a mountain in Olympic Park easy to hike and visually stunning. There are nearly 100 views of Three Mile Canyon, the Snyderville Basin, Canyons ski terrain, and the Utah Olympic Park.

Distance: 6.5 miles (10.5 km). Add about 0.5 mile (0.8 km) round trip from the bus or parking.

Elev. Gain: 1,190 feet (363 m)

Peak Elev: 8,033 feet (2,448 m)

Difficulty: *Intermediate.* There's a gentle climb the first 2.65 mi (4.3 km).

Configuration: Loop.

Note:

◊ See Hike #29 regarding the many amenities of Olympic Park.

◊ The lower *Moose Puddle Trail* has had some falling tree problems and may occasionally close.

◊ A view from this hike is on the front cover of this book.

DIRECTIONS:

- Ride to the Olympic Parkway and SR-224 **bus stop**. For free bus service to and within Olympic Park, inquire in the Visitor Center on the northwest corner of the intersection of Olympic Parkway and SR-224. It's a long, uphill walk for about 2 miles (3.2 km) from the SR-224 bus stop to the trailhead following directions given for drivers.
- **Drivers**, turn west off of SR-224 onto Olympic Parkway. Quickly come to a roundabout and proceed around 3/4 of the roundabout.
- Turn right (south) onto Olympic Parkway and proceed up this winding road.
- Pass Olympic Plaza and buildings on the left and find parking on the right, just before a road gate. Walk uphill past the gate and refrigerator buildings, and find a trailhead to the right as the road makes a horseshoe turn.

o   Turn right onto *Yeti's Trail* and follow it uphill. Ignore a few right forks as you near the top of the ridge. (Trails for practicing cyclists.) After coming over the top at about 2.6 miles (4.2 km), ignore a left fork to the very top, (unless you want to take it up and back down). Continue downhill and when you've gone about 2.75 miles (4.4 km) from the trailhead, ignore a right fork to *Olympic Trail*.

o   Continue downhill on *Moose Puddle Trail* through multiple switchbacks. Cross a dirt road three times to stay on the single-track trail and ultimately come to the paved road.

o   Turn left and walk down the road to parking or the bus at Olympic Plaza.

ROUTE SUMMARY:

o   On the Olympic Parkway, past the Olympic Plaza on the left, walk uphill past the gate and refrigerator buildings and find a trailhead to the right as the road makes a horseshoe turn.

o   Turn right onto *Yeti's Trail* and follow it uphill. Ignore a few right forks near the top, and a left fork to the very top. Continue downhill and ignore a right fork to the Olympic Trail.

o   Proceed on *Moose Puddle Trail*. Cross a dirt road three times to stay on the single-track trail and ultimately come to the paved road.

o   Turn left to return to start.

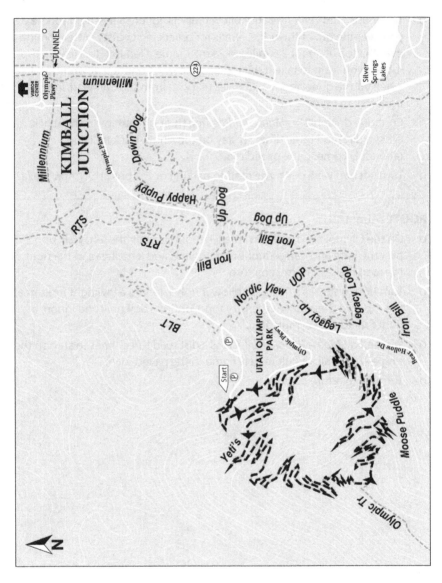

#28 Yeti's - Moose Puddle

#29 Olympic Park Loop

DESCRIPTION: Meander around or take part in the multiple, unique activities and adventures available in the Utah Olympic Park. This facility, the only one of its kind in the USA, serves America's top aerialist athletes, and provides bonuses for hikers.

Distance: 2.6 miles (4.2 km)

Elev. Gain: 480 feet (146 m)

Peak Elev: 7,422 feet (2,262 m)

Difficulty: *Intermediate.*
Switchbacks assist the climb. (A free bus to the top of Olympic Park may be available.)

Configuration: Loop.

Note:
◊ This hike takes you to Mountain Challenge, a free obstacle (Ninja) course.
◊ This route is easily combined with Hikes #30 and 31, the *Happy Puppy - Down Dog* and *RTS Trails*. There may be new trails here in the future.
◊ Utah Olympic Park, built for the 2002 games, is a 387-acre complex with training facilities for ski jumping, bobsled, luge, skeleton, and Nordic skiing. In summer, aerialists train and stage exhibitions by skiing off of ramps into a pool. Lessons and guided tours are available. A challenging climbing wall overhangs the pool.
◊ A free chairlift ride on the Freestyle Lift from the Nordic Plaza to the Olympic Plaza operates at peak times.
◊ Admission is free to the Alf Engen Ski History and the George Eccles 2002 Olympic Winter Games Museums, where you can experience a virtual chairlift ride, avalanche, and ramp jumping, along with film and exhibits. Restrooms are available in the museums.
◊ Olympic Park also provides for purchase: bobsled, zip line and extreme tubing rides, adventure courses, and training camps. Activity fees help support maintenance of this training center. Additional information about Olympic Park activities/events is available at *utaholympiclegacy.org.*

DIRECTIONS:

- Ride to the Olympic Parkway and SR-224 **bus stop**. For free **bus** service to and within Olympic Park, inquire in the Visitor Information Center on the northwest corner of the intersection of Olympic Parkway and SR-224. Directions for a reverse hike from the top of Olympic Park, accessible by bus, are given below.

- If park bus service is not available, it's a very uphill walk for about 1.7 miles (2.7 km) from the bus stop on SR-224 to the trailhead. Walkers and **drivers**, turn west off of SR-224, onto the Olympic Parkway. Quickly come to a roundabout.

- Proceed around 3/4 of the roundabout and turn south onto Olympic Parkway. If **walking**, proceed uphill to the Nordic Plaza.

- If **driving**, pass the Nordic Plaza and take the left turn past buildings into a parking area.

- From parking, walk east, downhill, past the museums and pool area to the Nordic Plaza, following signs to the Alpine Slide and Extreme Zip Line.

- From the Nordic Plaza, continue east past the ski jumps and around the bottom of the Nordic chairlift and Alpine Slide to arrive at a gravel road between two dirt trails.

- Take the dirt trail to the left of the gravel road. Proceed downhill for a short distance and come to a trail intersection with the *Iron Bill Trail*.

- Turn right onto *Iron Bill* and proceed through switchbacks to an intersection.

- Turn left at this intersection and proceed through more switchbacks. Ignore a left turn to *Up Dog Trail* and continue uphill to a fork to *UOP Trail*.

- Bear right at the fork and quickly come to an intersection with the *Legacy Loop Trail*.

- Turn right onto *Legacy Loop*, a single-track trail, and proceed through more switchbacks to a fork with *Legacy Ridge* to the left.

- Take the right fork towards *UOP Trail (Utah Olympic Park)*. Pass (or exit from) the Mountain Challenge obstacle course access trail on the left. Follow *UOP Trail* to pavement and a helicopter pad.

- Cross the helicopter pad. On its opposite side, find a dirt road through a break in the railing. Take this dirt road and quickly arrive at an intersection with *Nordic View Trail*.

- Turn left onto this single-track and proceed downhill. The trail will intersect with a dirt road three times. Bear left all three times. These junctions are marked by a fence, then a picnic table, and then an electrical utility box on the right.

- After a switchback, come to an intersecting trail and bear left back to Olympic Plaza where there is parking and hopefully, bus service. Alternatively you can walk downhill on Olympic Parkway to the bus stop on SR-224.

- **If you take the bus to the park top**, take *Legacy Loop Trail* and come to a fork.

- Bear right and come to an intersection.

- Bear right onto *UOP Trail* and come to an intersection.

- Bear left onto the *Iron Bill Trail*. Follow it to an intersection.

- Turn left onto a dirt road and arrive at the Nordic Plaza. Follow the paved road back to Olympic Plaza and Olympic Parkway.

ROUTE SUMMARY:

o From the Nordic Plaza in the Utah Olympic Park, pass the bases of the Nordic chairlift and Alpine Slide to arrive at a gravel road between two dirt trails.

o Take the dirt trail to the left. Proceed downhill for a short distance to an intersection.

o Turn right onto *Iron Bill Trail* and proceed through the switchbacks to an intersection.

o Turn left at this intersection and proceed through more switchbacks. Ignore a left turn to *Up Dog Trail* and continue uphill to a fork to *UOP Trail*.

o Bear right at the fork and quickly come to an intersection with *Legacy Loops*.

o Turn right onto the *Legacy Loop Trail* and proceed to a fork.

o Bear right towards *UOP* and proceed to a helicopter pad.

o Cross the helicopter pad and find a dirt road through a break in the railing.

o Take the dirt road and quickly bear left onto the single-track, the *Nordic View Trail*.

o Bear left onto single-track each time the trail intersects with a dirt road.

o After a switchback, come to an intersecting trail and bear left to return to start.

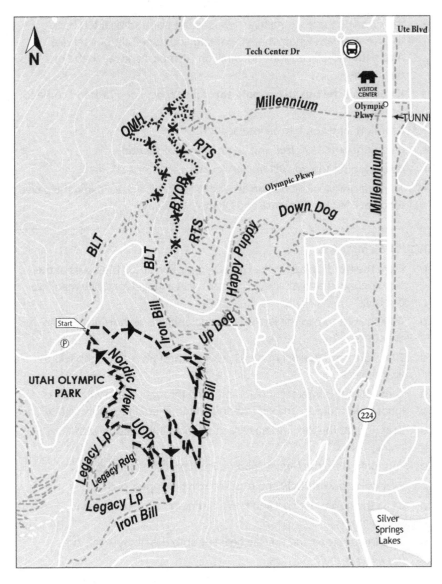

#29 Olympic Park Loop

#30 Happy Puppy - Down Dog

DESCRIPTION: Here are two short routes in 43 enclosed acres of open space for unleashed dogs and dog lovers. Formerly known as "Run-A-Muk" or "Bark Park," this terrain got some new names in 2019.

Distance: 1.3 miles (2.1 km) or 1.8 miles (2.9 km)

Elev. Gain: 138 feet (42 m) or 194 feet (59 m)

Peak Elev: 6,698 feet (2,042 m)

Difficulty: Very *easy*.

Configuration: Loops.

Note:

◊ This route is easily combined with Hike #31 RTS and #29 Olympic Park Loop. Connect with Olympic Park via the *Up Dog Trail*.

◊ There are **rules** for this leash-free dog area:

- Use the leash free area at your own risk. Owners are responsible and liable for the actions of their dog(s).
- Dogs must be leashed while entering and upon leaving the fenced area.
- No more than three dogs per adult.
- Dogs must wear valid rabies and license tags.
- Children under 15 years of age must be supervised at all times.
- Conducting professional dog training or holding special events is prohibited without permission from Basin Recreation.
- Parking area is open from dawn to dusk.
- Clean up after your pet.

NOT allowed are:

- Puppies less than four months old
- Sick or aggressive dogs
- Dogs in heat
- Choke/prong or pinch collars
- Alcohol or smoking
- Bicycles

DIRECTIONS (ROUTE SUMMARY):

- If you are hiking without a dog, this area is approachable from the *Millennium Trail* along the west side of SR 224, just south of the Visitor's Center in Kimball Junction and the Olympic Park and SR 224 **Bus Stop**.

- Since Rover is not allowed on the bus, directions are given for **drivers** from the Run-A-Muk parking area in Olympic Park. From SR 224, turn west onto Olympic Parkway, just south of the Visitor's Center. Quickly come to a roundabout.

- Proceed 3/4 of the way around the roundabout and turn right onto Olympic Parkway.

- Just after the second road curve, find parking on the left. Enter through the gates and turn right onto *Happy Puppy Trail*. Ignore a right turn to a culvert and ignore the right fork to *Up Dog Trail*. Continue to a three-way intersection.

- For the shorter loop, **Route A**, turn left onto *Happy Puppy Trail* at this intersection, and left again at the next intersection to return to start.

- For the longer loop, **Route B,** turn right at the intersection onto *Down Dog Trail* and proceed until you come to a four-way intersection.

- Proceed straight and arrive at another three-way intersection.

- Proceed straight at this intersection, veering to the left to return to start.

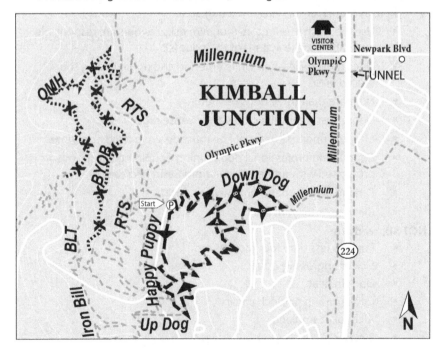

#30 Happy Puppy - Down Dog

#31 RTS

DESCRIPTION: Follow a winding trail through Kimball Junction fields and aspen groves.

Distance: Route A 3.6 miles (5.8 km). Route B 2.3 miles (3.6 km)

Elev. Gain: 262 feet (80 m), more by bus.

Peak Elev: 6,763 feet (2,061 m)

Difficulty: *Easy.* Very gentle inclines.

Configuration: Loop.

Note:
◊ This route is easily combined with Hike #29 in Olympic Park and Hike #30 Happy Puppy - Down Dog.
◊ Directions are numbered to identify two routes.

DIRECTIONS (AND ROUTE SUMMARIES):

Route A:
- Ride to the Olympic Parkway and SR 224 **bus stop.** From the bus stop, walk south on the paved *Millennium Trail* a short distance to a four-way intersection.
- Turn right onto an intersecting paved trail heading west. Come to left forks that take you to a dirt single-track trail. Turn right onto the single-track from any of the forks and then follow the directions numbered 5, 6, 7 and 8 for Route B, but at direction 9, bear left, ignoring the right fork to parking. Then follow directions 2 and 3. Arrive at any of the right forks back to the paved *Millennium Trail*.
- Bear right onto *Millennium* and follow the pavement south, back to SR 224.
- Turn left to return to the bus stop.

Route B:
1. **Drivers** turn west off of SR 224 onto the Olympic Parkway. Quickly come to a roundabout and follow it 3/4 of the way around and turn south onto Olympic Parkway. Just after a second road curve, pass a left parking area and find a parking area on the right. Turn right to park.
2. From the parking area, bear right onto the *RTS Trail*.

3. Quickly come to two three-way intersections and turn right at both.
4. Ignore a few forks onto a double-track, staying on the single-track switchbacks.
5. Stay left at a right footpath and at two more right forks to the paved *Millennium Trail.*
6. Ignore a right fork for "downhill bikers only," and ignore three more right forks.
7. At a left fork followed by a right fork, stay straight on the single-track.
8. Ignore a wide left fork to another single track, staying high.
9. Ignore right turns onto the *BYOB Trail* and then the *BLT Trail.* Stay left.
10. At a three-way intersection, take the left fork. Proceed to a right fork to parking,

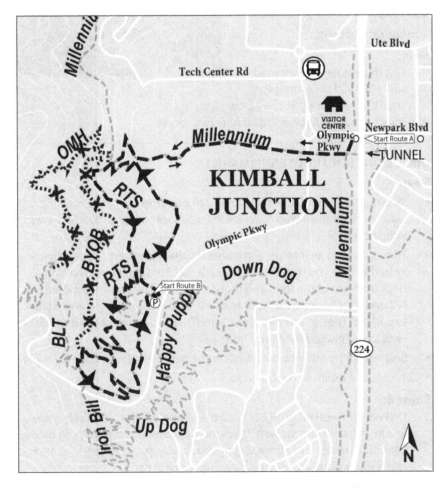

#31 RTS

#32 Road to WOS - Over Easy

DESCRIPTION: A shady pine forest, fields of sunflowers and balsamroot, lookout benches, and gorgeous scenery make this route well worth the effort.

Distance: 4.4 miles (7.1 km)

Elev. Gain: 1,172 feet (357 m)

Peak Elev: 8,524 feet (2,598 m)

Difficulty: *Difficult.* Be prepared to climb for about 1.7 miles (2.7 km), starting off steeply. Surface is rocky in places and descent requires attentive footwork. Look for orange paint markings at confusing trail intersections and where there are hazardous stumps or steps.

Configuration: Loop.

DIRECTIONS:
- There is **no bus** service to this trailhead, though there is a Summit Park bus stop that would put you on Aspen Drive. However, following driver instructions would mean climbing an additional 600 feet (183 m) for an additional 1.75 miles (2.8 km).
- **Driving** from Park City, take I-80 west to exit 140, Summit Park. (Going west on I-80 from Park City, this is the second Summit Park exit.)
- Turn left off the exit ramp crossing under the highway.
- Take the first right turn after the highway onto Aspen Drive/Maple Drive. Proceed to an intersection with Parkview Drive.
- Turn left on Parkview. Ascend this winding road to limited trailhead parking, just before Parkview merges into Matterhorn Drive.
- Walk around the trailhead gate and proceed to an intersection showing *Short Ribs* and *Road to WOS Trails* to the left. Turn right onto a double-track, the *Water Tower Upper Trail.*
- Proceed uphill. Ignore a left fork to the *Lower Water Tower Trail* and come to a three-way intersection. *Short Ribs Trail* is to the right.
- Turn left toward the *Road to WOS Trail* and quickly come to a three-way intersection.
- Turn right and continue uphill to a four-way intersection.
- Cross the *Road to WOS Trail* bearing left and make an immediate right turn onto the *Over Easy Trail.*
- Proceed uphill. After a big climb with switchbacks, the trail comes to a fork.
- Bear left and continue uphill, and arrive at what seems like a high point with a right fork.

- To **detour**, take the right fork and follow the trail up the ridge where it bends right. After about a hundred yards (meters) uphill, behind a big tree, find a bench dedicated to Craig Patterson, an avalanche forecast professional, killed by an April 2013 avalanche.
  - To return to *Over Easy*, retrace your steps down from the ridge and turn right.
- Continue along *Over Easy* and you can pass or take another detour right fork.
  - This short **detour**, *Summit Slam*, climbs to a lookout. Then return the way you came to *Over Easy* and turn right.
- Continue downhill on *Over Easy*. There will be a left fork to ignore, and you'll come to an intersection with *Road To WOS Trail*.
- Pass this intersection. Quickly come to a left turn, *Over Easy Trail*.
- Turn left and continue downhill on *Over Easy* to another intersection with *Road to WOS*.
- Turn left onto *Road to WOS*. Continue to a fork.
- Bear right onto *Side Order Trail* and continue downhill to another intersection.
- Bear right, back onto *Road to WOS*. Follow it through switchbacks to another intersection.
- Turn right to return to trailhead parking.

ROUTE SUMMARY:

o In Summit Park, at the merge of Parkview Drive with Matterhorn Drive, pass the trailhead gate and proceed to an intersection.

o Turn right onto a double-track, the *Water Tower Upper Trail*.

o Proceed uphill. Ignore a left fork and come to a three-way intersection.

o Turn left toward *Road to WOS* and quickly come to a three-way intersection.

o Turn right and continue uphill to a four-way intersection.

o Turn left and then immediately turn right.

o Proceed uphill to a fork.

o Bear left and continue uphill. Arrive at a high point with a right fork to a detour. Bear left here, and bear left at the next detour fork to *Summit Slam Trail*. Continue along *Over Easy* downhill. Ignore a left fork and come to an intersection with *Road To WOS Trail*.

o Pass the intersection, and shortly after, come to another intersection.

o Turn left and continue downhill to another intersection.

o Turn left and continue to a fork.

o Bear right onto *Side Order Trail* and continue downhill to another intersection.

o Bear right onto *Road to WOS* and follow it to another intersection.

o Turn right to return to start.

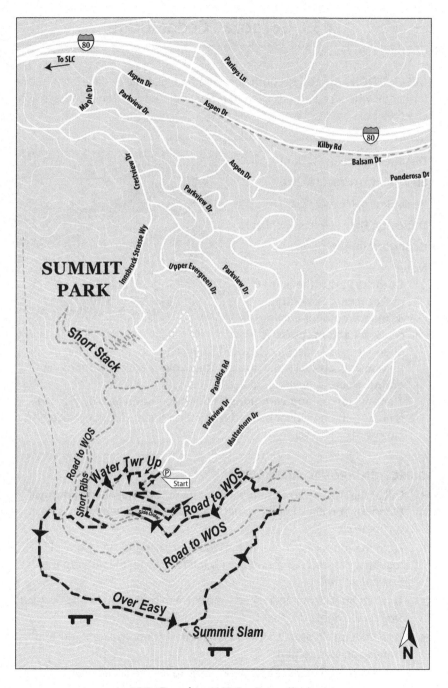

#32 Road to WOS - Over Easy

#33 Gorgoza - Cedar Ridge

DESCRIPTION: Appreciate both the wild and gentrified sides of this land formation where cedar trees cling to rocky ridges and extreme athletes exercise their passions.

Distance: 2.6 miles (4.2 km)

Elev. Gain: 336 feet (102 m)

Peak Elev: 6,736 feet (2,053 m)

Difficulty: *Easy* due to switchbacks.

Configuration: Lollypop.

Note:

◊ **Gorgoza Park** is the home of **Woodward Park City**, an indoor/outdoor training center for **action sports**. It offers lift-assisted technical cycling, skiing and tubing, and jump ramps, trampolines, obstacle courses, and other unique athletic options, plus **dining**. woodwardparkcity.com

◊ There are lots of **loop variations** for this hike. The *Road to Arcylon* loop is not recommended for hikers due to cyclist traffic. (Arcylon spelled backwards = No Lycra)

DIRECTIONS (ROUTE SUMMARY):

- Exit at the Woodward **bus stop**, where there's also trailhead **parking** at Woodward on Kilby Road, just north and west of the Jeremy Ranch exit on Route 80.

- From the southwest corner of the Woodward parking, find a gravel road that passes a pond, and quickly intersects with the public paved *Millennium Trail*.

- Turn left on Millennium. Proceed about 1/4 mile (0.4 km) to find *Gorgoza Trail* on the right.

- Turn right on *Gorgoza*. Follow the switchbacks. Ignore a right fork and come to an intersection.

- Proceed straight. Ignore a left fork. Come to an intersection with *Pinebrook Point Connector*.

- Turn left onto the *Connector* and come to a 3-way intersection.

- Bear left and come to a T- intersection.
- Turn left, heading downhill. Ignore a right footpath, ignore a left fork, and then ignore a steep footpath on the left and come to the road, Cedar Court.
- Turn left and proceed to an intersection with Cedar Drive.
- Turn right and proceed to an intersection with Pointe Drive.
- Turn left and proceed to another intersection with Cedar Drive.
- Turn left. Descend on Cedar to the paved *Millennium Trail* just before Kilby Road.
- Turn left onto *Millennium* to return to Woodward. (There's also the option of taking the bus back from the Cedar Drive bus stop on Kilby Road.)

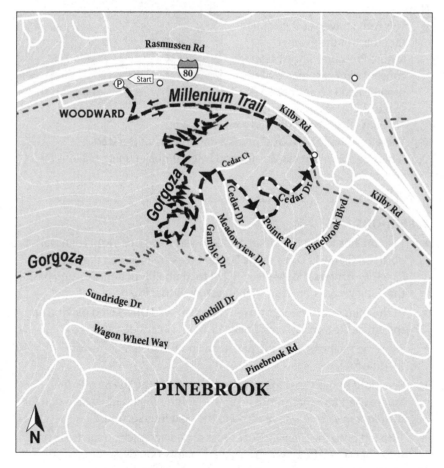

#33 Gorgoza - Cedar Ridge

#34 Glenwild - Blackhawk

DESCRIPTION: Springtime was made for a sunny stroll in the hills that perch above Spring Creek. It's a Disneyland for birders and geologists.

Distance: 3 miles (4.8 km)

Elev. Gain: 336 feet (102 m)

Peak Elev: 7,422 feet (2,044 m)

Difficulty: *Easy* due to switchbacks.

Configuration: Loop.

Note:

◊ This route traverses the wildlife sanctuary of the Swaner Nature Preserve. Since 1995, conservation easements here protect 1,200 acres of open space, 800 acres of wetlands, 10 miles (16 km) of trails, and a historic farm.

◊ There's no shade here, but there's a dog "beach" at the start.

◊ A hillside spine of rocks was formed by earthquake uplift, millions of years ago.

DIRECTIONS:

- Take the bus to the Bitner Road at Glenwild Drive **bus stop**. Then walk north on Glenwild Drive to the Spring Creek Trailhead on the left. From Park City, **drivers** should take SR-224 to Kimball Junction, proceed past the I-80 overpass, and turn right (east) on Bitner Road.

- At the third intersection, turn left onto Glenwild Drive. Find parking on the left at the Spring Creek Trailhead, or on Creekside Lane.

- From the trailhead, take the path to "all trails." Quickly come to a triangle fork.

- Bear right uphill. Cross the road and proceed along the *Stealth Trail*. Ignore a left fork that comes up at the eighth switchback, with a sign for the *Blackhawk Trail, and* proceed to the next intersection.

- Turn left onto the *Glenwild Trail*. Cross a road and pick up the trail on the other side. After passing a spine of pointy boulders, come to an intersection.

- Turn left onto the *Blackhawk Trail* and continue to another intersection.
- Bear right onto *Blackhawk Drop Trail*. Come to an intersection with *Stealth Trail*.
- Turn left onto *Stealth* to return to the trailhead.

ROUTE SUMMARY:

o   Start at the Spring Creek Trailhead on Glenwild Drive. Take the first right fork and cross the road to ascend on *Stealth Trail*. Come to a second intersection.

o   Bear left onto *Glenwild Trail*. Cross the road and continue to an intersection.

o   Turn left onto *Blackhawk Trail* and continue to the next intersection.

o   Turn right and continue to the next intersection.

o   Turn left back onto *Stealth Trail* to return to start.

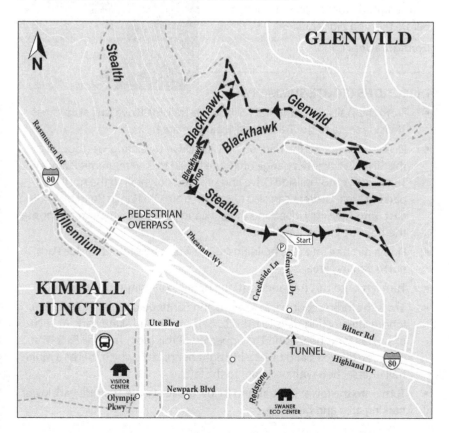

#34 Glenwild - Black Hawk

#35 Trailside Park Loop

DESCRIPTION: This short, easy hike is one of several routes provided by Trailside Park, a 63-acre community facility that also features playgrounds, sports courts, an off-leash dog trail and dog parks, a skateboard park, picnic areas, and a technical bike park that offers thrills for spectators as well as for cyclists.

Distance: 1.1 miles (1.8 km)

Elev. Gain: 110 feet (34 m)

Peak Elev: 6,690 feet (2,039 m)

Difficulty: *Easy.* This is a good place to test altitude tolerance and stamina before tackling bigger hikes.

Configuration: Loop.

DIRECTIONS (ROUTE SUMMARY):

- From the Trailside Elementary School on Trailside Drive **bus stop**, cross Trailside Drive to the Trailside Park parking area.
- **Drivers** can access the park on Trailside Drive by exiting westbound at the Silver Creek interchange on Route US-40 to Silver Summit Parkway. Turn north onto Trailside Drive and proceed downhill to the north parking area. **Drivers** can also approach from Old Ranch Road by turning east onto Trailside Drive. Find the park and parking on the right opposite the Trailside Elementary School.
- Find a dirt trail after the buildings at the west end of the Trailside Park north parking area.
- Turn left onto this trail and continue uphill to a multi-trail intersection.
- Cross the intersection to go straight and continue on the *TSP Loop Trail*. Ignore intersecting trails to the disc golf course and skate park. At each of six trail forks bear right. The upper leg of this loop, *Trailside Park West*, crosses a dirt road and takes a big right bend, after which there's a multi-trail intersection with two trails to the left.
- Turn onto the lower left trail and follow it back to the Trailside Park lower parking area and bus stop.

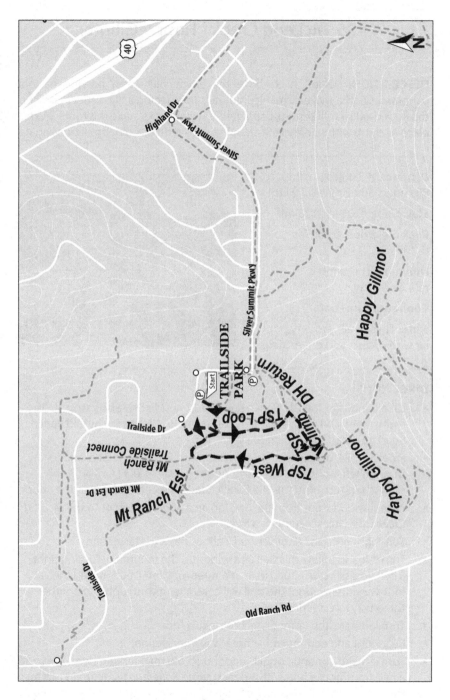

#35 Trailside Park Loop

#36 McLeod Creek - Happy Gillmor

DESCRIPTION: Rolling hills above the Snyderville Basin provide pastoral panoramas and a maze of manicured trails in a geologically distinct corner of the Round Valley trail system. Long gentle switchbacks make this route an ideal place to climb with minimal effort, but you'll need this guidebook to navigate.

Distance: 4.3 miles (6.8 km).
Bus riders add 2 miles (3.2 km).

Elev. Gain: 420 feet (128 m)

Peak Elevation: 6,890 feet (2,100 m)

Difficulty: The climb is relatively *Easy.*

Configuration: Loop.

Note: These trails are very popular with cyclists and equestrians.

DIRECTIONS:

- Take the bus to the Old Ranch Road and Trailside Drive **bus stop**. Walk south along Old Ranch Road for about a mile (1.6 km) to the Old Ranch Road trailhead parking on the left.
- From SR-224, **drivers** should turn east onto Old Ranch Road, and follow through left, right, and left turns. About 0.2 miles (0.33 km) after the second left turn, find the Old Ranch Road trailhead parking on the right.
- Ascend stone steps from the parking area and bear left onto the *McLeod Creek Trail*. Quickly come to a fork.
- Turn right onto the *Rambler Trail*. Follow it to a T-intersection.
- Turn left and follow this trail as it winds up the mountain, turning right three times: first at a fork, then at a three-way intersection, and then at a four-way intersection. The trail will continue to wind uphill to another three-way intersection.
- Turn left here and immediately come to a fork.
- Bear right and continue to a three-way intersection.
- Turn left and continue uphill, ignoring an old road forking right. Arrive at a five-trail intersection with a bench along *Rademan Ridge Trail*. Look for the *TM Trail* to your extreme left, almost parallel to the *Rambler Trail* you just ascended.

- Turn sharply left onto the *TM Trail*. Follow through about fifteen switchbacks and twenty-one crossings of old roads, some rocky and some grassy. Stay on the single-track dirt trail, taking a left fork at the fifteenth switchback to arrive at a sign at a seven-way intersection.
- Turn extremely left (switchback #16) onto *Happy Gillmor Trail,* heading west and then south.
- Just after the first switchback on *Happy Gillmor,* arrive at a four-way intersection.
- Turn left and immediately arrive at another four-way intersection.
- Turn left. Continue around a big switchback curve to arrive at another four-way intersection.
- Go straight and arrive at an X-intersection.
- Turn left, but not extreme left, and proceed to another four-way intersection.
- Proceed straight, following around another big switchback curve, and across a dirt road. Arrive at another X-intersection.
- Turn right, but not extreme right. Ignore the next right fork, cross a rocky road, and arrive at a three-way intersection.
- Bear right and continue to another fork.
- Bear right to return to the Old Ranch Road trailhead.
- Bus riders turn north (right) on Old Ranch Road to return to the bus stop.

ROUTE SUMMARY:

o From the Old Ranch Road trailhead, bear left (north) onto the trail. Quickly come to a fork.

o Bear right onto *Rambler Trail*. Come to an intersection.

o Turn left and bear right at the next three intersections.

o Wind uphill to another three-way intersection.

o Turn left and immediately come to a fork.

o Bear right. Continue to a three-way intersection.

o Turn left and ignore a right fork. Continue uphill to a five-way intersection.

o Turn sharply left onto *TM Trail* and follow through fifteen switchbacks and multiple road crossings. Take a left fork at the fifteenth switchback to arrive at a sign at a seven-way intersection.

o Turn extremely left (switchback #16) onto *Happy Gillmor*. Arrive at a four-way intersection.

o Turn left and quickly arrive at another four-way intersection.

o Turn left and come to another four-way intersection.

o Go straight and arrive at an X-intersection.

o Turn left, but not extreme left, and proceed to another four-way intersection.

o   Proceed straight, cross a dirt road, and arrive at another X-intersection.
o   Turn right, but not extreme right. Ignore the next right fork, cross a rocky road, and arrive at a three-way intersection.
o   Bear right and continue to another fork.
o   Bear right to return to start at the Old Ranch Road trailhead.

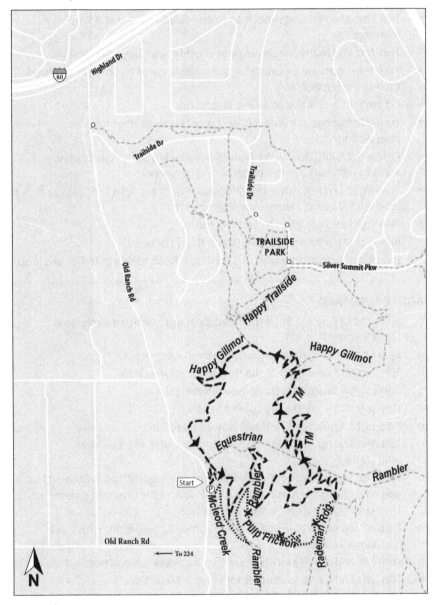

#36 McLeod Creek - Happy Gillmor

#37 RV Connect - Silver Quinns

DESCRIPTION: The northeast corner of Round Valley is a favorite of cyclists and equestrians, but enjoyable for hikers too. View ski terrain and the hillside homes of Promontory.

Distance: 3.3 miles (5.3 km).
Add 0.8 miles (1.3 km) for bus riders.

Elev. Gain: 289 feet (88 m)

Peak Elev: 6,864 feet (2,092 m)

Difficulty: *Easy.* Ascents are gentle.

Configuration: Loop.

DIRECTIONS:

- Ride to the Highland Dr and Sagebrook Dr **bus stop** and walk south on Highland to the trailhead. **Drivers** exit off of US-40 onto Silver Summit Parkway at the Silver Creek exit. Turn left (west) off the exit ramp, cross over the highway and make the first left turn onto Highland Drive.
- Walk or drive south along Highland for 0.4 miles (0.6 km), to a trailhead at the end of the road. Find parking to the left. Walk west on a path with homes to the right, and utility poles to the left. Between the second and third utility poles, find a dirt single-track trail on the left.
- Turn left onto *RV Connect.* Beware of cyclists and come to an intersection.
- Turn left again. Ignore some left forks to a dirt road above you. Come to an intersection.
- Cross the dirt road to stay on *RV Connect.* Continue to a fork.
- Bear left onto *Ramble On Trail.* Continue through switchbacks to a fork.
- Turn left onto the *Rusty Spur Trail.* Proceed to the paved *Silver Quinns Trail.*
- Turn left onto *Silver Quinns* and follow it back to Highland Drive.

ROUTE SUMMARY:

o   From the Highland Drive trailhead, walk west. Find a trail between the second and third utility poles on the left.

o   Turn left onto *RV Connect Trail* and come to an intersection.

o   Turn left and proceed to a dirt road. Cross the road and pick up *RV Connect* on the other side. Continue to a fork.

o   Bear left onto the *Ramble On Trail* and continue to a fork.

o   Turn left onto *Rusty Spur Trail*. Proceed to the paved *Silver Quinns Trail*.

o   Turn left onto *Silver Quinns* to return to start.

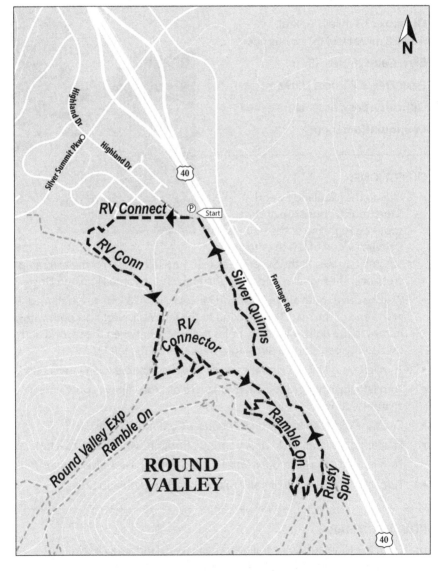

#37 RV Connect - Silver Quinns

#38 Valderoad - Somewhere Elks

DESCRIPTION: Highlands and lowlands offer all sorts of landscapes along these trails that loop through the preserved open space of Round Valley. Bluebirds and other wildlife love this terrain.

Distance: 5.6 miles (9 km), more for bus riders.

Elev. Gain: 526 feet (160 m), more by bus.

Peak Elev: 7,132 feet (2,430 m)

Difficulty: *Intermediate*. Ascents are long but relatively gentle.

Configuration: Loop.

DIRECTIONS:

- Unless bus service expands to the northeast corner of Park Meadows, expect a 1.25 mile (2 km) uphill walk from the Evening Star and Little Kate **bus stop**. From the bus stop, proceed east on Little Kate to Lucky John Drive and turn left.

- **Drivers** turn north off of SR-248 onto Monitor Drive and proceed to the first intersection with Lucky John Drive and turn right.

- Lucky John becomes Meadow Drive. Follow it to Sunny Slopes Drive.

- Turn right on Sunny Slopes. Proceed to the second left hand turn, Fairway Hills Court.

- Turn left onto Fairway Hills. Turn right onto Round Valley Way to trailhead parking. (Big bump upon entrance.)

- After checking trailhead notices, take the trail next to the bulletin board. This trail, *Matt's Flat*, heads north and right, and arrives at a fork.

- Bear right towards *Matt's Flat* and *Ability Way* and bear left at the next fork, continuing on *Matt's Flat*. An unmarked single-track trail will come up on the left.

- Bear left onto this single-track which ascends a short way to *Valderoad Trail*.

- Bear left onto *Valderoad* and continue past intersections with *Nowhere Elks, Downward Dog, Barrel Roll*, and the *Seventy 101 Trails*. Arrive at a fork with the *Round Valley Express Trail,* which *Valderoad* merges into.

- Bear right onto *Round Valley Express*. Proceed to a major intersection.

- Bear right onto *Rambler Trail* which quickly forks to *Ramble On Trail*.
- Bear right to continue on *Rambler* through multiple switchbacks. Come to a fork with *Seventy 101 Trail*.
- Bear left to stay on *Rambler* and arrive at a four-way intersection with *Rusty Shovel* and *Nowhere Elks Trails*.
- Bear right onto *Nowhere Elks*. At intersections with *PorkUclimbTrail, Barrel Roll Trail, and Downward Dog,* bear left to stay on *Nowhere Elks*. Arrive at an intersection with *Somewhere Elks Trail*.
- Bear left onto *Somewhere Elks* and arrive at an intersection with *Rambler*.
- Turn right onto *Rambler* and it will quickly intersect with *Matt's Flat*.
- Bear right on *Matt's Flat*. Past the *Valderoad* intersection, the trail merges with *Ability Way*. Quickly veer left back onto *Matt's Flat*. Come to an intersection with *Fast Pitch Trail*.
- Turn right onto *Fast Pitch,* which returns to the trailhead and parking on Round Valley Way.
- Leaving the trailhead, turn left and then right to get to Meadows Drive. Bus riders turn right on Little Kate Road. Drivers continue to Monitor Drive to get to SR-248.

ROUTE SUMMARY:

o   From the trailhead on Round Valley Way, take the trail next to the bulletin board, *Matt's Flat*. Quickly arrive at a fork.

o   Bear right towards *Matt's Flat* and *Ability Way* and bear left at the next fork onto *Matt's Flat*. Proceed to an unmarked single-track trail on the left.

o   Turn left and ascend to the *Valderoad Trail*.

o   Turn left onto *Valderoad*. Pass intersecting trails and come to a fork with *Round Valley Express Trail*.

o   Bear right and arrive at a multi-trail intersection.

o   Bear right onto *Rambler Trail* and come to a fork.

o   Bear right. Continue uphill through switchbacks to an intersection.

o   Bear right onto *Nowhere Elks Trail* and continue to an intersection with *Somewhere Elks*.

o   Bear left onto *Somewhere Elks*. Come to an intersection with *Rambler*.

o   Turn right onto *Rambler,* which quickly intersects with *Matt's Flat*.

o   Bear right onto *Matt's Flat*, which will merge into *Ability Way Trail*. Continue briefly and bear left back onto *Matt's Flat*. It quickly intersects with *Fast Pitch Trail*.

o   Turn right onto *Fast Pitch* to return to start.

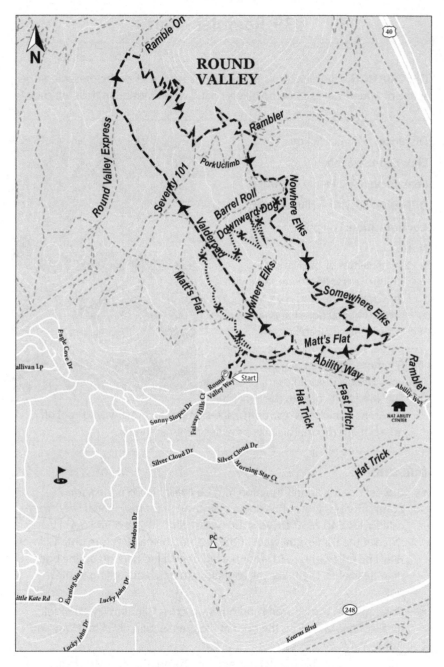

#38 Valderoad - Somewhere Elks

#39 Rambler - Kari's

DESCRIPTION: This hike through the southeast corner of the preserved open space of Round Valley can keep hikers hiking when mountain trails are snowy.

Distance: 3.1 miles (5 km)

Elev. Gain: 228 feet (69 m)

Peak Elev: 6,932 feet (2,113 m)

Difficulty: *Easy.* The climb is gentle.

Configuration: Lollipop.

Note:

◊ The facilities of the National Ability Center (NAC) network with these trails. The NAC is a non-profit organization that enables individuals of all abilities to participate in sport and recreation. For more information go to *www.discovernac.org*.

◊ This hike starts next to the Park City Ice Arena (which has restrooms). Ice-skating is a great way to cool off on a hot afternoon. This hike provides minimal shade.

DIRECTIONS:

- **Bus** service to Quinn's Junction may be available from the Kamas Commuter bus line or bus riders may arrange for free shared service by calling 435.640.7819. **Drivers** turn west off of SR-248 onto Round Valley Drive at the traffic light west of US-40. Take the first left turn onto Gillmor Way and follow this road around a big bend. Find parking on the right near ball fields. Then take the asphalt path north of parking to the ice rink.

- Coming from the ice arena and bus stop, cross Gillmor Way, and look for the *Rambler Trail* on the right at the intersection of Gillmor Way and Ability Way.

- Turn right onto this trail. It crosses over a footpath and a dirt road. Proceed to a fork.

- Bear right to stay on *Rambler*. Come to a switchback with intersecting trails.

- Take the trail to the far left. Proceed through more switchbacks and come to another fork with the *Ramble On Trail*.
- Bear left to stay on *Rambler*. Proceed across a dirt road and come to a four-way intersection.
- Turn left to stay on *Rambler* and arrive at a three-way intersection.
- Turn to the extreme left onto *Kari's Trail*. Cross a road and come to a three-way intersection.
- Turn left to stay on *Kari's*. Ignore a left footpath after a bend and proceed to a three-way intersection.
- Proceed straight (right) onto *Rambler Trail* again. Continue to a three-way intersection with *Somewhere Elks Trail*.
- Turn left to stay on *Rambler* and proceed to a fork.
- Bear left and continue to the end of the trail across from the ice arena and bus stop. Drivers can walk south from the ice rink on a paved path back to parking.

ROUTE SUMMARY:

o   Find *Rambler Trail* on the northeast corner of the intersection of Gillmor Way and Ability Way.

o   Turn right onto *Rambler*. Cross a footpath and a dirt road. Proceed to a fork.

o   Bear right to stay on *Rambler*. Come to a switchback with intersecting trails.

o   Take the trail to the far left and come to another fork with the *Ramble On Trail*.

o   Bear left to stay on *Rambler*. Cross a dirt road and come to a four-way intersection.

o   Turn left to stay on *Rambler* and arrive at a three-way intersection.

o   Turn to the extreme left onto *Kari's Trail*. Cross a road and come to a three-way intersection.

o   Turn left to stay on *Kari's*. Proceed to a three-way intersection.

o   Proceed straight (right) onto *Rambler Trail* again. Continue to a three-way intersection.

o   Turn left to stay on *Rambler* and proceed to a fork.

o   Bear left to return to start.

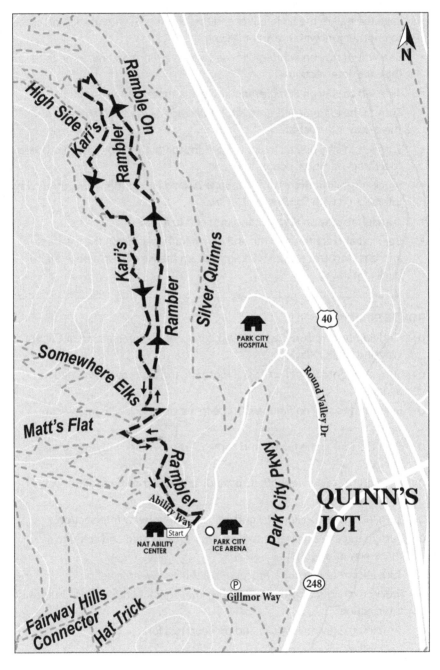

#39 Rambler - Kari's

#40 Matt's Flat - Cammy's

DESCRIPTION: Short and superbly scenic, this route steers you through the maze of trails that occupy the southwest corner of the protected open space of Round Valley.

Distance: 2.4 miles (3.8 km), more for bus riders.

Elev. Gain: 343 feet (105 m), more by bus.

Peak Elev: 7,083 feet (2,159 m)

Difficulty: *Easy.* Switchbacks make for a mellow ascent, but navigation is tricky.

Configuration: Loop.

DIRECTIONS:

- Unless bus service expands to the northeast corner of Park Meadows, expect a 1.25 mile (2 km) uphill walk to the trailhead from the bus stop on Little Kate Road at Evening Star Drive. From the bus stop, walk east on Little Kate to an intersection with Lucky John Drive.

- Turn left onto Lucky John. It turns into Meadows Drive. After a second climb and big bend to the left, find the Cove trailhead on the right.

- **Drivers** can get to the Cove trailhead by turning east off of SR-224 at the intersection of Meadows Drive. Proceed up a long hill and look for the Cove trailhead parking on the left, before the road bends sharply south.

- From the trailhead, take the rocky *Round Valley Express Trail* uphill. Ignore a left turn and come to a fork.

- Bear right towards *Matt's Flat Trail* and come to another fork.

- Bear left and continue to a three-way intersection.

- Bear right to continue on *Matt's Flat* and arrive at an intersection with the *Backslide Trail.*

- Bear right onto *Backslide* and continue uphill through switchbacks. After a lookout bench on the left, the trail crosses a dirt road. Continue straight around a horseshoe bend to a triangular multi-trail intersection.

- Bear right at the triangle and then straight onto a downhill double-track trail (*Matt's Flat* again) in the direction of the *Seventy 101 Trail*. Proceed to another trail intersection.
- Bear left onto *Cammy's Trail* and continue to four-way intersection.
- Continue straight on *Cammy's* and proceed to another four-way intersection.
- Proceed straight again on *Cammy's* and continue to a triangular three-way intersection.
- Bear right and continue to a fork.
- Bear left, continuing in the direction of the *Rademan Ridge Trail* and quickly come to another multi-trail intersection.
- Bear left, continuing on *Cammy's Trail*. Come to a three-way intersection with *Lah Dee Duh Trail*.
- Turn left and proceed to a fork.
- Bear right to return to the Cove trailhead and parking.
- Bus riders walk south on Meadows Drive. It becomes Lucky John Drive. Turn right onto Little Kate Road. Proceed to the Evening Star and Little Kate bus stop.

ROUTE SUMMARY:

o   From the Cove Trailhead, take the rocky uphill trail. Ignore a left turn. Come to a fork.

o   Bear right towards *Matt's Flat Trail* and come to another fork.

o   Bear left and continue to a three-way intersection.

o   Bear right to continue on *Matt's Flat* and arrive at an intersection with the *Backslide Trail*.

o   Bear right onto *Backslide* and continue uphill to a multi-trail intersection.

o   Bear right and then straight onto double-track, *Matt's Flat*. Come to another intersection.

o   Turn left onto *Cammy's Trail* and continue to a four-way intersection.

o   Continue straight on *Cammy's* and proceed to another four-way intersection.

o   Proceed straight again on *Cammy's* and continue to a three-way intersection.

o   Bear right and continue to a fork.

o   Bear left and quickly come to another multi-trail intersection.

o   Bear left, continuing on *Cammy's Trail* and proceed downhill to the *Lah Dee Duh Trail*.

o   Turn left and proceed to a fork.

o   Bear right to return to start.

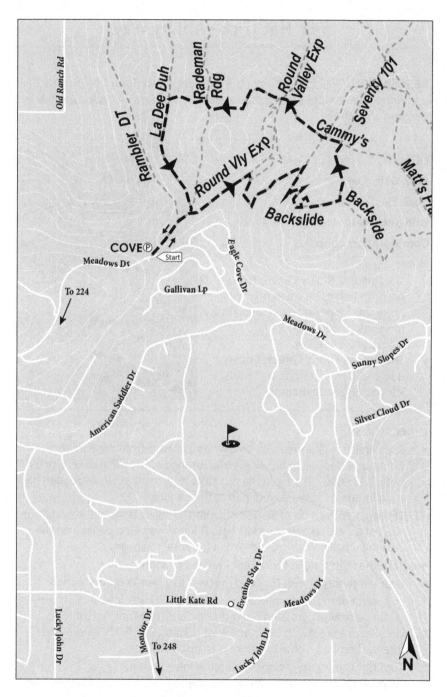

#40 Matt's Flat - Cammy's

#41 Hat Trick - Ability Way

DESCRIPTION: Circling facilities of the National Ability Center, these wide trails accommodate athletes on foot, horseback, bikes, adaptive cycles, snow-bikes, skis, and snowshoes.

Distance: 2.2 miles (3.5 km)

Elev. Gain: 206 feet (63 m)

Peak Elev: 6,892 feet (2,101 m)

Difficulty: *Easy* with a gentle climb.

Configuration: Loop.

Note:

◊ The National Ability Center (NAC) pastures horses here and provides programs for disabled persons. For more information go to *www.discovernac.org*.

◊ The Quinn's Sports Complex offers dog parks, playgrounds, ball fields, ice skating and restrooms.

DIRECTIONS:

- **Bus** service to Quinn's Junction may be available from the Kamas Commuter bus line or bus riders may arrange for free shared service by calling 435.640.7819. From the bus stop, walk south on a paved path past a playground. Cross a paved road to the trailhead.
- **Drivers** turn west off of SR-248 onto Round Valley Drive at the traffic light west of US-40. Take the first left onto Gillmor Way. Find parking on the right near ball fields, across the road from the trailhead.
- Take the right trail, *Hat Trick Trail*. Proceed to a fork.
- Bear left to stay on *Hat Trick* and proceed to a four-way intersection.
- Turn right onto *Fast Pitch Trail*. Proceed to a four-way intersection and continue straight, crossing *Fairway Hills Connector Trail*. A right fork detours to a tire swing. Continue west (left) on Fast Pitch. Ignore a left intersecting trail. Come to a right turn opposite a bench.
- Turn right and quickly come to another intersection.
- Turn extremely right onto *Ability Way Trail*. Ignore intersecting trails and arrive at a paved road. Just before the road, notice a narrow footpath to

the right, *Rambler Trail*.

- Drivers should turn right onto *Rambler* and follow it to a dirt road, *Fairway Hills Connector*.

- Turn left on this road into a utility area and quickly arrive back on paved Gillmor Way across from the parking.

- Bus riders can arrange for Dial-A-Ride, and instead of turning right on *Rambler*, stay on *Ability Way* to arrive back at the ice rink bus stop.

ROUTE SUMMARY:

o   From the Quinn's trailhead, turn right onto *Hat Trick Trail*. Proceed to a fork.

o   Bear left to stay on *Hat Trick*. Come to a four-way intersection.

o   Turn right onto *Fast Pitch Trail*. Proceed to a four-way intersection and continue straight on *Fast Pitch* until you come to a trail on the right, opposite a bench.

o   Turn right and quickly turn right again onto *Ability Way Trail*. Follow it to a paved road to return to the bus stop. Just before the road, drivers can find the *Rambler Trail* to the right.

o   Turn right onto *Rambler,* and follow it to a dirt road,

o   Turn left on this road to arrive on paved Gillmor Way and parking.

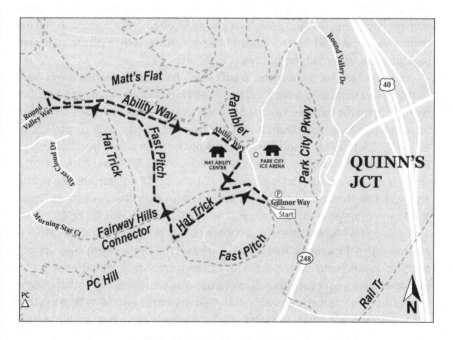

#41 Hat Trick - Ability Way

Hiking with Kids, Dogs, or Alone

Children may prosper the most from hiking. Getting kids away from electronic screens and outdoors are obvious benefits. But the added benefits of "family time," the opportunity to befriend your child with nature, and the challenge and sense of accomplishment and confidence provided by the hiking experience, are probably the best reasons to get them out on the trails.

If your child has been exposed to hiking by others, and is encouraging you to take a hike with her, make sure you're fit enough to engage in this sport: Learn safety basics as explained in this guidebook. Become familiar with terrain before taking kids there. Know basic first aid. Know the children and their stamina levels. Respect the child who doesn't want to hike, and make other arrangements for that child. Some kids are timid and overwhelmed by new experiences, and need gradual introductions to what others consider an inviting adventure.

If you're a hiking parent, trying to get your young ones into this sport, here's some advice about hiking with infants and young children.

For **infants** and **toddlers** with **limited walking** ability:

Don't fret about taking your newborn for a hike. Human babies have been carted around in slings, papooses and other carrying contraptions since humans have been walking upright. It's never been easier to "kangaroo" a baby than now. Some child carrier options have rain/sun hoods, a diaper changing pad, and special pockets for bottles, phones, etc.

For babies **under six months, a soft shell, front sling carrier** works best, enabling you to monitor your little one. The extra weight in front is good counterbalance for the extra weight in your backpack, now full of diapers and other traveling baby supplies. From about **six months** of age, and 16 pounds of weight (7.3 kg) on up, a **solid frame backpack** carrier works best, so long as the baby can sit up with good head and neck control. The maximum weight a child carrier should support is probably 40 pounds (18 kg), assuming a strong adult can tote that much weight, along with water and other necessities. Some child carriers are advertised to support as much as 50 pounds (23 kg).

If an adult is hiking alone with a baby, a desirable feature of a child carrier is a frame with a "**kickstand**" that allows you to set the carrier down in an upright position. This is particularly helpful for loading, unloading, and attending to a fussing child or your own needs. Such frames may be heavier than others. Some frames are foldable. Look for well-padded straps and adjustability features that allow different size adults to switch off. Trying the backpack on with the child in it is the best way to select a comfortable model that will not spoil the hiking experience for parent or passenger.

Acclimate your baby to the carrier before embarking on a hike. Try short easy walks in comfortable weather to see how it goes. The rhythmic motion of walking has a good chance of putting an infant to sleep, so timing your hike with your baby's nap may work well for you both.

Even if you breastfeed and drink plenty of water yourself, bring a bottle of extra water along and offer the baby water periodically. A wide brimmed hat should protect your little one's face and eyes from direct sunlight. A blanket can also protect from sunburn or wind.

Pack an adequate number of diapers and plastic bags to haul them out. If your child produces poop that is too yucky or voluminous to carry, you can bury it in a **cat hole** as described for adults in the chapter on responsible hiking on page 9.

For **preschoolers**: (Ages 3-5 years) and children too big to carry:

Hiking may or may not be a good activity for this age group, depending on the individual child. Some kids in this age group are highly mobile and agile, but have no judgment or sense of danger. Some are extremely curious and want to touch and climb on everything, but are not well coordinated. Some should not be out on trails unless they are wearing a harness and **leash**. One family member may have to totally devote the hike to managing one active child, and such a plan should be clear to everyone involved. If there's **good communication**, there shouldn't be a situation where a parent says, "I thought *you* were watching him." Stitching up lacerations and casting broken bones in weekend urgent care clinics for a few decades, I heard those six words too often.

It's important to keep babies and young children **hydrated, fed** and at a **comfortable temperature**. Like adults, they should be dressed in layers that are easily added, subtracted, and carried. (See the gear chapter regarding hiking clothing.) The use of "cute" water carriers can encourage kids to drink. Little ones need about 1-2 cups (0.25-0.5 L) of water per hour. Many children will do best with a water bladder backpack system; more accessible and less easily spilled than water bottles. Stopping and playing or resting in the shade can prevent overheating. Scarfs and gloves can provide non-bulky warmth.

UV protection for children requires appropriate sunglasses, hats, and sunscreen. Please read the chapter on sun, sight and skin.

Young hiking children should do fine wearing well-fitting sneakers. Young feet grow quickly. Shoe size and wear and tear should be monitored monthly. Check for adequate toe room and that the heels do not slip when they walk up steps. Make sure there's enough tread to provide traction. Double knot shoelaces to prevent tripping.

The real challenge of hiking with young children is keeping them **motivated**. Select easy trails and give them frequent breaks. Let them explore and climb on logs and boulders while you carefully supervise. Give them a snack when they get to the next switchback, or the next intersecting trail, or the next time the sun hides behind a cloud. Give them some tasks as in the textbox examples.

Embellishing a trail experience with fantasy can also keep young children motivated. Unless you are ethically against lying to a child, an older sibling or parent can walk ahead and leave a favorite treat on a visible log or rock. The four-year-old might be persuaded that a "trail fairy" leaves little bags of goldfish crackers for good hikers, or the "hiker's hero" leaves hot wheels cars at the trail's end. A special treat after a hike might be motivating for next time.

Please bear in mind throughout your hike, that small children out on trails should never appear separated from adults, especially at dawn and dusk when wildlife is more active. Predatory animals are amazingly adept at singling out the easiest prey, like the dawdling youngster in the back of the herd.

For **school aged young children** (Ages 5-10 and maybe preteens):

Including them in selecting a destination, planning a hike, packing their own pack and snacks, and allowing them to bring a friend can stimulate interest. Each child should be given a **whistle** and instructed in how to use it if ever separated from the family (e.g. two toots, then count to ten and toot again). If you have a child who shows interest in trees, birds, bugs, or the like, hiking can provide a learning lab and offer numerous opportunities to teach children about maps, animals, plants, weather, caring for the environment, safety, the buddy system, sunburn, poison ivy, staying hydrated, and numerous other life skills. For some children, hiking can be an opportunity to talk, sing, or tell stories. Taking pictures can motivate a budding photographer. Some children enjoy scavenger hunt activities. Decorating a paper bag to put their collection

Sample Preschooler Activities

- Can you find a yellow flower? A blue one?
- Who sees a bee? A butterfly? A chipmunk?
- Who hears a bird? An airplane?
- How many rocks are in that pile?
- Does that rock feel cold or hot?
- Does that flower smell?
- Which is the tallest tree? The fattest?
- Find a pointy leaf. Find a round one.
- Is this a grape or a berry?
- Why shouldn't we eat these berries?
- Are we going uphill or downhill?
- Is it sunny? Shady? Cloudy?
- Which way is the wind blowing?
- Can you find a good walking stick?
- Etc.

Sample: Scavenger Hunt
- A feather
- Three different colored rocks
- A rock with a hole in it
- A seashell (there are marine fossils on basin trails)
- A pinecone
- A green leaf, a brown leaf, red, etc.
- Something shiny, sparkly, fuzzy, twisted, bumpy, smelly
- Etc.

in before a hike, may add appeal. A virtual scavenger hunt might entail giving each youngster a checklist to note their observations rather than physically collect them.

Children might enjoy being challenged to compete in using their senses. Who's the first one to see an animal? Hear a bird? Notice when the wind changes direction? Who can taste the wind on their tongue or find the best smelling flower? Can you make your fingers smell like pine or like sage? Which tree has the smoothest bark?

A resting exercise might be to identify everything between Trees A and B. How many colors are there? How many shades of green? How many kinds of plants? Are there bugs? What kind of an animal might live here? Who can take the silliest picture sitting on a tree stump?

Try assigning each child a different "job" on different hikes. One can carry binoculars and be bird watcher. Another can be safety officer, trail blazer, snack coordinator, or dog master. Another can be "drink master" and remind everyone to take frequent sips of water. Keeping scrapbooks of their hikes will stimulate some children. Some children will only need positive reinforcement to enjoy hiking. And some children will hate hiking and will need to be channeled into activities more in keeping with their abilities and preferences.

Geocaching may motivate tech-savy kids. This is a high-tech kind of treasure hunt that involves the use of a Global Positioning System (GPS) or other navigational device or technique to hide and seek "caches". A **cache** can be a container of goodies or a beautiful place. The Swaner Nature Preserve in Park City's Kimball Junction sponsors geocaching adventures. Find information at *www.swanerecocenter. org*. (Utah is a major geocaching destination and boasts one of the world's largest GeoTours. Check it out at *www.visit.utah.com*.)

Hikes in this guidebook that may be suitable for youngsters were

Sample: Virtual Scavenger Hunt
- Moss, a fern, a cactus
- A specific tree or flower
- A specific bird or butterfly
- A cricket, spider, ladybug, etc.
- A squirrel, chipmunk, rabbit, etc.
- A bird's, squirrel's, or wasp's nest
- Bird or insect holes in a tree
- Sounds of a woodpecker
- Lightning scar on a tree
- Animal fur on a tree
- Avalanche trees
- A branch shaped like an alphabet letter
- A cairn, a boulder, a rock quarry
- An antler, an anthill
- Animal tracks
- Etc.

selected because they are relatively short, easy, or have other features to make the outing more interesting. If you're unsure if your child is ready to hike, you may want to check out my previous book, *Park City Walking Guide,* which identifies eleven child-friendly walks in parks and neighborhoods, and on easy trails, like those around the Deer Valley Duck Ponds. You can get the benefits of being outdoors as a family and getting exercise, without some of the challenges of hiking. (You can access the Duck Pond trails in conjunction with Hikes #s 5, 6, 7, and 8 in this guidebook.)

Ten Possible Park City Hikes for Youngsters							
#	Hike Name	Mi	Elev Gain Ft	km	Elev Gain m	Extra Attractions (Cautions)	Rest Rooms
35	*Trailside Park Loop*	1.1	110	1.8	34	Play grounds, skate park, sports courts, bike park	A few in the park
24	*McPolin Farm Nature Trail*	1.7	195	2.7	59	History, vintage farm equipment, and environmental education	Building behind barn
40	*Olympic Park Loop*	2.6	480	4.2	146	Free museums, obstacle course, aerialist shows, thrill rides and more	Museums
30	*Happy Puppy -Down Dog A*	1.3	38	2.1	42	Easily combined w/ the Olympic Park (but kids have to like dogs – this is a leash-free dog park.)	Drive to Olympic Park
	Happy Puppy -Down Dog B	1.8	194	2.9	59		
31	RTS	2.3	262	3.6	80	Can also combine with Olympic Park	Ditto
41	*Hat Trick - Ability Way*	2.2	206	3.5	63	Ice rink, ball fields, playground, dog park, National Ability Center	Ice rink, ball fields
39	*Rambler - Kari's*	3.1	228	5	69	Ditto	Ditto
2	*Empire Pass - Silver Lake*	2.2	120	3.5	37	Bus ride up, hike down. Deer Valley Resort amenities	Lodge at end of hike
5	*Silver Lake - Tour De Homes*	2.7	23	4.4	7	Ditto, plus some cool trailside sculptures	Lodges at both ends

Hiking with dogs is almost never a matter of motivation. Rover is usually the most eager hiker in the family. Unfortunately, his eagerness can get him into all kinds of trouble on trails, so it is recommended that hiking dogs be leashed. **Park City requires all dogs to be leashed in public places except designated leash-free areas.** Owners of free-running dogs can be fined. A shepherd, rancher or ranger can **legally kill a dog** that chases or harasses farm animals or wildlife. Be aware that flocks of sheep are occasionally herded through Park City's mountains, and goats have been employed for weed control for some ski terrain. What are the odds that your dog wouldn't want to chase a lamb or a goat? If in a leash-free zone, dogs must be obedient and reliably voice controlled. If not, they can easily be injured or killed by a fast-moving cyclist or skier, or a wild animal.

Dog owners must appreciate that some people who've had a bad dog experience may be petrified of our beloved pets. It may also be true that dogs sense when people don't like them, which might make them act more aggressively towards that already scared person. Even in the case of a sweet, friendly dog who just jumps up to greet a person who doesn't like dogs, the owner of the unleashed dog can be held liable for any injuries the victim might claim. Moreover, just like children, some dogs are innately cautious, while others are reckless and manage to get into trouble wherever they go, in spite of obedience training. Some such dogs should probably never be off-leash for their own safety.

All dogs should wear a collar with **identification**. Park City officials also recommend that unfriendly dogs wear a yellow ribbon or bandana on their collar or leash to warn others. The **yellow-dog project** helps nervous dogs, and prevents bites to dog lovers who might otherwise approach an animal that needs to be left alone.

Before even considering hiking with your dog, make sure she is old enough, healthy enough, and is adequately protected with vaccinations. Let your vet know your dog is out on the trails, so appropriate immunization is advised. Make sure Rover is fit enough and not too old himself. Make sure his toenails are trimmed so they don't catch on stuff. Start him out on easy hikes before tackling harder ones. Labored breathing or slowing down could be signs of serious problems. Rest and reverse direction if rest doesn't help.

Know some doggy first aid and be observant of your dog's behavior. Did he drink pond water? Eat a pinecone or a dead mole? The vet needs to know to make the best decisions if Rover becomes ill. Ticks and fleas, intestinal worms, and diseases like rabies can be contracted by dogs from interaction with other dogs or wild animals. Dogs can catch the distemper virus from raccoons and skunks. Mosquitoes can transmit heartworm disease. Dogs can pick up the giardia parasite from drinking stream water and infect their human family. You owe it to your pet and selves to provide the best protection possible.

Just like humans, hiking dogs need **adequate amounts of water**. If none is available along the trail, as is true for most of the hikes in this guidebook, either you or the dog needs to take some along. A big dog needs ½ to 1-ounce (15-30 ml) of water per pound (0.5 kg) per day, more if he's very active and it's hot. A small dog, <20 pounds (9 kg), needs more, about 1.5 oz (45 ml) of water per pound (0.5 kg) per day. Visualize a 60-pound (27 kg) retriever needing two quarts (2 L), for a 6-8 mile hike, about as much as their human companion; the 20 pound corgi needs 1 quart (1 L). The thing about free-running, active young dogs is if you go 5 miles (8 km), they probably meander 10 (16). **Dog backpacks** can accommodate collapsible nylon water bladders, dishes, food, treats, poop bags, and other gear. Make sure the pack fits your dog and acclimate Rover to carrying a loaded pack at home before you expect him to put up with it on the trail. He shouldn't carry more than 25% of his body weight.

UV protection for dogs is available in the form of sunglasses, goggles, and hats and visors that accommodate dog ears. If you can get your dog to tolerate any of these, you might **delay the development of cataracts**. Dogs with **pink noses** sunburn easily and get cancers. They would do well to tolerate a long visor or glasses with a nose shield. Some dog owners are probably snickering as they read this; their pooch would never tolerate such a getup. But if they had the chance to raise another young pup to be a hiking buddy, wouldn't it be good to acclimate her to wearing a hat to protect her vision. Special sunscreens for pink noses, bald spots and other skin issues are also available.

Dogs overheat easily. They shouldn't be hiking in temps greater than 85° F (29° C). If there's no shade at all, they shouldn't be hiking in temps near that range. Small dogs close to the ground, and black dogs, shouldn't be hiking on blacktop surfaces when it's hot. Burned paw pads are painful and disabling. So are frozen paw pads. Some dog booties provide thermal protection, while others are tough enough to protect Rover's feet from sharp rocks.

Unlike humans who perspire, it's difficult for a dog to cool off once overheated. Symptoms of heat stroke include anxious behavior, heavy panting, excessive drooling, and hyperventilating (heavy breathing). This can progress to organ failure and death, so prevention is the key. Cooling bandanas marketed to runners may benefit Rover. These are reusable cloth wraps filled with special crystals that retain coldness after refrigeration.

Wildlife encounters are another danger for dogs. Bears, moose, elk, coyotes, mountain lions, bobcats, and rattlesnakes all pose serious risks. So does any mama animal protecting babies. One of my hiking, unleashed dachshunds was once swooped by an enormous owl that probably decided not to fly off with her in his talons, only because my other dog and I were a few steps behind. Keeping Rover leashed is the best way to prevent a disaster. **Leashes** should be no longer than 6 feet (1.8 m) in length and able to withstand a hard pull. Retractable type leashes may not survive a dog that wants to chase a deer. Never allow a small dog to appear separated from people. Pick it up if a coyote or other predator is present.

Amongst the things the dog pack might store are **basic first aid supplies** and for the typical dog, that starts with **tweezers** to remove thorns, cactus spines, foxtails, ice crystals, pebbles, and other little things that get caught between toes. A limping dog should be promptly checked for **foot problems** that can be readily resolved by removing a foreign body or piece of ice. A paw protecting **bootie** in the first-aid pack is a decent remedy for a cut foot, if Rover is too big to carry. Sometimes, just wrapping a cut paw in a bandana will keep him from walking on it, until you can get the wound proper attention.

Dogs like to hunt in rocky crevices and rotted out logs. Unfortunately, those are the same places that skunks, porcupines, hornets, and other beasties build their nests. **Antihistamines** are useful first-aid for a dog stung by bees or fire ants. Figure a dose of diphenhydramine (Benadryl®) at about 1 mg/pound (0.5 kg), every 12 hours. So, a 25 lb (11 kg) dog gets a 25 mg tablet, but 50 mg is the most a big dog should get, even if he weighs much more. That is the adult human dose. Do not use extended release capsules for dogs. If Rover is shaking his head, sneezing a lot, or shows eye discharge, get him to the vet.

Should your dog ever get quilled by a **porcupine**, it is imperative to try to **get the quills out promptly** or they migrate inward where they can cause serious long-term problems. You cannot simply pull porcupine quills out because there are barbs on the ends that can cause terrific pain and tissue damage. Quills have to be taken out with pliers, using a twisting motion, and general anesthesia is typically required to remove quills from the nostrils, tongue and palate of the pup who tried to bite the porky. If Rover has quills in his feet and he's too big to carry, call for help.

If your pooch gets **skunked,** immediately flush the eyes and blot up any of the oily musk you can see on Rover's fur. Promptly wash him

**Recipe for Skunk
Musk Removal Solution
For Dog Fur**
1 qt. (1 L) 3% Hydrogen Peroxide
¼ c. (60 cc) baking soda
1 tsp. (5 ml) dishwashing liquid

Leave on 3-5 minutes
Avoid eyes, ears, nostrils, and mouth

For a small dog
2 c. (0.5 L) 3% Hydrogen Peroxide
2 Tb. (30 cc) baking soda
½ tsp. (2.5 ml) dishwashing liquid

with the recipe noted here, or vinegar diluted in water, or tomato juice out of the can. Lather up the fur in areas where he was sprayed and leave the solution on for 3-5 minutes. Keep the solution out of eyes and rinse thoroughly with plain water if the eyes are contaminated. Also keep the solution out of ears, nostrils and the mouth. Wear rubber gloves to bathe the dog, preferably outdoors. There are also proprietary products for removing skunk odor, which you might want to keep on hand if your too curious pooch gets repeatedly skunked.

One more item to toss in Rover's backpack, if he's got a good amount of fur, is a brush to remove cobwebs, leaves, and whatever else snarls in his coat, before he jumps in the car. This is also a good time to check for ticks.

Some of the hikes in this guidebook favor dogs and some hikes may not be ideal for dogs as noted in the accompanying tables. Willow Creek Park on Old Ranch Road, (not included in this guidebook), provides a dog pond, a park, and a dog agility course.

Hikes That FAVOR Dogs	
30 Happy Puppy -Down Dog Rts. A & B	These trails are in a leash-free dog park
34 Glen Wild - Black Hawk	Starts with a dog beach
35 Trailside Park Loop	Leash-free dog park within Trailside Park
36-41 Round Valley Trails	Since 2016, some trails are designated leash-free on a trial basis. Obey signs.
39 Rambler - Kari's	Leash-free dog park at Quinn's Junction
41 Hat Trick - Ability Way	Ditto

Hikes That DISFAVOR Dogs	
4 Silver Lake - The Lookout	Long staircases with serrated metal steps
9 Sultan Out & Back	Too many horses
15 Sweeney's - 4:20	Long staircases with serrated metal steps
29 Olympic Park Loop	Leashed dogs are permitted but too much for people to do here
32 Road to WOS - Over Easy	Intersects back country Salt Lake County where dogs are not permitted

Hiking alone:

I encounter many lone hikers with dogs on Park City trails, but also many people who **hike alone.** I do too. I enjoy the solitude, though I also enjoy meeting people and dogs along the way. I relish going at my own pace and stopping to watch a bird or admire a flower, without holding up companions. I've been fortunate to encounter mostly wonderful people on the trail. Occasionally, I'm annoyed by clueless cyclists who sneak up behind me, but I've never yet met on a trail, the kind of person who made me wish I had a little canister of mace or a penknife in my hand. Still, I think there are things lone walkers can do to improve their safety in addition to being vigilant.

As for all sports and recreational activities, being knowledgeable, conditioned, experienced, and prepared for all contingencies is the best way to insure safe participation.

If possible, learn a hike in the company of others before going it alone. Select popular hikes at peak times so other people are around. Wear a police whistle on a lanyard. Stay alert. Get away from anyone who makes you uncomfortable, even if it means changing direction or latching on to other hikers. Don't share your itinerary with someone you meet on the trail, but be very sure someone at home knows where you're going and when you expect to be back. A website called *alltrails.com* offers an app that allows someone to remotely track your hike.

If you really don't want to be alone out there, and have no reliable hiking companion, consider joining a hiking club or get a dog. And if you can't have a dog, there are more than a few too-busy, dog-loving people who will gladly pay for dog-hiking services for their under-exercised pet. Maybe it's your neighbor's kids who need a hiking companion. On page 184 of this guidebook, find information about local and nearby hiking clubs.

Hiking alone, or hiking with kids and dogs can make the experience all the more rewarding. Even if you're only motivated to get the kids outdoors or exercise the pooch, everyone benefits.

Altitude, Health, and Exercise

Old Town **Park City rises about 7,000 feet (2,134 m) above sea level**. Some of the walks in this guidebook are at elevations of 8,000-10,000+ feet (2,438-3,048+ m). Although this is the low end of the high altitude spectrum, it's still high enough to impact how some humans may feel or perform. This chapter explores some of what is known about the effects and potential risks and benefits of high altitude exposure for **visitors, residents**, and **athletes**.

High altitude medicine is a relatively new specialty in which few physicians have training. Limited research is often based on the effects of very high altitude on pilots or experienced mountain climbers, while the effects of more moderate elevations on ordinary people are less well studied.

Modern transportation brings folks who live at low elevations to high altitude in just a few hours. With ascent this rapid, as many as **1 in 4 adults** may experience high altitude symptoms, even at moderate elevations if engaging in strenuous exercise. One study identified altitude symptoms in 1 of 3 of traveling children and adolescents, but other studies suggest their risk is lower. There's a genetic predisposition to being altitude intolerant, and certain health conditions increase the risk of adverse reactions to high altitude. Therefore, persons who **plan to travel to Park City** and hike, ski, or partake in other physical activities, should **become familiar with the symptoms of high altitude illness (HAI),** especially if coming from below 3,000 feet (914 m) elevation.

The primary cause of **HAI** is inadequate oxygen, (**hypoxia**). While the amount of oxygen in the air (21%) doesn't change as one climbs mountains, the atmospheric (barometric) pressure steadily decreases as one goes up. Think of atmospheric pressure as the "weight" of air, or the little bubbles in this illustration. Air gets "heavier" as it approaches sea level. The higher up on Earth's surface you climb, the "lighter" air becomes. "Lighter" (low pressure) air diffuses less oxygen to the lungs than does heavier air.

People unaccustomed to high altitude lose about 1% of their respiratory capacity for every 328 feet (100 m) they ascend above c. 5,000

feet (1,500 m). Thus, an elevation of 8,202 feet (2,500 m) reduces breathing efficiency by about 10% for healthy, but not yet acclimated persons. The body has several ways to compensate for low oxygen. Chemical receptors detect the lower oxygen level in blood and send signals to stimulate faster, deeper breathing, (**hyperventilation**). Hypoxia also stimulates the heart to beat faster, and the peripheral blood vessels to dilate to bring more blood to the tissues. Many people never notice these acclimatization adjustments, but dilated blood vessels in the brain are probably the cause of **high altitude headache.**

After a few days at high altitude, these compensatory mechanisms increase the oxygen supply to tissue and symptoms lessen. After two to three weeks at the higher elevation, the body produces more red blood cells to increase the amount of oxygen the blood can carry. Once the blood becomes "oxygen-richer", a person can exercise with less shortness of breath, a slower heart rate, and less fatigue with exertion. This is called **acclimatization.**

Classification of High Altitude		
Degree	**Feet**	**Meters**
High	*8,000-12,000*	*2,438-6,358*
Very High	*12,000-18,000*	*3,658-5,486*
Extremely High	*>18,000*	*>5,486*
Mount Everest	*29,035*	*8,850*

HAI (High Altitude Illness)

There are several forms of high altitude illness. The most common is **Acute Mountain Sickness (AMS).** Going from low to high elevation in less than a day can bring on symptoms, the first of which is often headache, sometimes severe. Other common symptoms like nausea are noted in the text box (on the next page). **Babies** with AMS may show fussiness, loss of appetite, and decreased sleeping. AMS symptoms can start within a few hours of ascent, and often persist for three days. Symptoms are worst the first night and tend to improve over two to three days. If AMS symptoms start to develop, do not ascend any higher, avoid strenuous exercise, and keep well-hydrated.

Park City has a dry climate and visitors can easily dehydrate. **Dehydration is commonly mistaken for acute mountain sickness**. Symptoms of dehydration and AMS are similar, especially the headache and fatigue. Some of the body's water supply is released into the air with every exhalation, seen as steam in cold weather. In hot dry weather, a great quantity of fluid can be lost through hard breathing and perspiration, and sweat evaporates so quickly in the dry air, it may go unnoticed. If a visitor also drinks coffee, tea, colas, some sports drinks, etc., the **caffeine** in these beverages further increases fluid loss through increased urination (**diuresis**), as does drinking **alcohol.** Caffeine withdrawal can also cause headaches, but with or without caffeine, visitors should make it a

Common Symptoms of AMS
Headache
Fatigue, weakness
Loss of appetite
Nausea, vomiting
Dizziness
Disturbed sleep
"Hangover" feeling in the morning
Swelling of the hands and feet

point to consume much more water than they normally do at lower altitudes.

Local ski patrollers too often find vigorous, young athletes "crumped" along high trails, looking as pale as the snow. These visitors arrive from sea level after a 90-minute flight, and an hour later, they're trying to ascend to the resort peak. Some are too nauseous to drink the water needed to be revived, and require intravenous hydration. Feeling better after rehydrating with a pint or two (½-1 L) of water can help distinguish symptoms of acute dehydration from symptoms of acute mountain sickness. A dehydrated person's symptoms will ease with replenishing water, but symptoms of AMS will persist until descending to a lower elevation.

When high altitude illness is suspected, **going to a lower altitude is the first line of treatment**. Descending about 1,000 feet (305 m) will often relieve AMS symptoms. The Park City Hospital is equipped to handle high altitude emergencies, but its elevation is about 6,891 feet (2,039 m). In a non-emergency situation, descending a few thousand feet (meters) to Salt Lake City, with an average elevation of 4,327 feet (1,320 m), could be the better remedy. Mild symptoms will usually resolve within a day of resting at lower altitude. A quicker option is to head to Heber City, about 20 minutes to Park City's south. The Heber Valley Medical Center's altitude is 5,604 feet (1,708 m), but dinner in a Heber restaurant with two to three big glasses of water, may be all the treatment that's needed. Headache can be treated with an over-the-counter NSAID such as ibuprofen or naprosyn, but these drugs can aggravate nausea. Acetaminophen may be effective for headache without the risk of nausea. Avoid aspirin.

If descending to lower altitude is not possible or helpful, oxygen administration is the next treatment. At-risk visitors may want to obtain a precautionary prescription for supplemental oxygen from their personal physician before travel. Local companies can deliver oxygen and equipment to hotels. If descent to a lower altitude and supplemental oxygen do not stop symptoms, emergency medical care is recommended.

Disturbed sleep, without other AMS symptoms, may be a variant of AMS. Visitors to high altitude commonly report difficulty falling asleep, frequent nighttime awakenings, and feeling tired in the morning. With some Park City hotel rooms above 8,000 feet (2,438 m), altitude sensitive persons might want to consider lodging options based on elevation. Sleeping in Salt Lake City and playing in the mountains can work well for some AMS prone persons.

If a sufferer of AMS ignores worsening symptoms, not only might they ruin a family vacation, but they put themselves at risk for more dangerous, potentially fatal forms of high altitude illness, including swelling of the brain (cerebral edema), and accumulation of fluid in the lungs (pulmonary edema).

High altitude cerebral edema, (HACE), is very unlikely to occur at Park City elevations. Although AMS usually precedes it, HACE sometimes develops without warning. Symptoms include **confusion** and **loss of coordination**, progressing to **inability to walk,** usually within 48 hours of arrival. Seek immediate emergency room care if suspected.

High altitude pulmonary edema (HAPE) also tends to occur at altitudes higher than Park City, starting around 13,000 feet (4,000 m), and usually after 48-72 hours. The first symptoms of HAPE are **reduced exercise capacity, shortness of breath** and a **dry cough**. If an affected person doesn't descend when such symptoms occur, shortness of breath worsens, there's difficulty lying flat, coughing may produce blood, and lips, fingernails, and then the skin start to look blue (**cyanosis**). Cerebral edema may also develop. Like HACE, **HAPE can be fatal without prompt intervention.** If HAPE develops below altitudes of c.10,000 feet (3,000 m), there could be an unidentified, underlying lung or heart problem needing urgent medical attention. Some risk factors for respiratory problems at moderate altitudes include marked obesity, acute respiratory infection, sleep apnea, and restriction of chest wall motion due to neuromuscular disease.

The good news about **HAI** is that it's **both preventable** and **treatable** if promptly recognized. Individuals who have previously had symptoms of AMS, or who have a family history of any form of HAI, are at increased risk and should **take extra precautions**.

For healthy people without a personal or family history of HAI, there's no practical way to know whether or not they may be adversely affected by travel to high altitude, other than experience. **Being physically fit is not preventive** for the genetically at-risk.

People who suffer from high altitude sensitivity can avoid trouble by **ascending slowly**. This may mean spending the first night in Salt Lake City before arriving in Park City, or sleeping at the lower elevation and limiting high altitude activity such as hiking or skiing to daytime hours. Staying well-hydrated and avoiding alcohol are highly recommended. Not engaging in strenuous exercise on the first day at higher altitude may also prevent AMS.

In the case of an individual with known susceptibility to HAI, who does not have the time to acclimate slowly, a prescription medication called **acetazolamide, (Diamox), can prevent the development of AMS**, when taken in advance. A trial of acetazolamide before travel is prudent to make sure it's well tolerated. Acetazolamide should not be taken in pregnancy or in persons with sulfa allergy. There are other prescription options, and limited evidence that over-the-counter naprosyn or ibuprofen might also prevent AMS. In persons at risk for pulmonary edema, prescription nifedipine or dexamethasone may prevent **HAPE.** Consult your personal physician before traveling if you have heart or lung problems.

Other Biologic Effects of Altitude

Though not an illness, **high altitude flatus expulsion, (HAFE),** is a possible consequence of rapid ascent. Yes, this is a discussion of farts, known amongst American mountain climbers as the "tude toots" or "Rocky Mountain barking spiders." Although some would argue that Park City is not elevated enough to cause HAFE, a combination of beer and beans, along with rapid ascent on ski lifts, could make HAFE a problem for some Park City visitors, or for the people sharing a gondola with them.

HAFE occurs because the volume of a gas in a container will expand if external pressure on the container is reduced. (A balloon expands if you stop squeezing it: **Boyle's Law**.) Remember that atmospheric pressure decreases as altitude increases, so gas in the intestines will expand as one ascends from Salt Lake City to Park City and the outside air pressure decreases. The expanding volume of gas stimulates

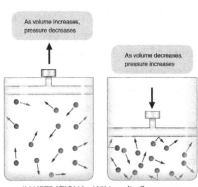

ILLUSTRATION by Wikimedia Commons

the intestines to contract and push the gas out in bigger volumes and more frequently than normal. [Normal adult intestinal gas production is about half a quart (1/2 liter) a day.] Also, in the first few days at high altitude, low oxygen levels increase the amount of carbon dioxide in the blood, which diffuses into the intestines to make them even gassier. Using digestive enzymes (beano) or simethicone (which absorbs gas), may reduce the risk of HAFE, as can strategic eating.

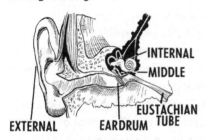

EXTERNAL — EARDRUM — INTERNAL — MIDDLE — EUSTACHIAN TUBE

ILLUSTRATION by wpclipart.com

Rapid changes in altitude are also associated with **pressure changes** in the **ears** and **sinuses**. This is especially true for air travel and riding ski lifts, but hikers can also be affected. Behind the eardrum is an air-filled cavity, the middle ear, which connects with the throat by an air-filled canal, the Eustachian tube. The sinuses are cavities in the facial and skull bones that fill with air from the nose. (Sinuses are not well developed until adolescence.) When a healthy person breathes, the inhaled air circulates into the Eustachian tubes, middle ears, and sinuses. This keeps the air pressure equal between these spaces and the outside atmosphere.

If the free flow of air is blocked, air pressure inside these cavities may become greater than the pressure of the outside atmosphere as one ascends, (Boyle's law again). Expanding air can cause a sense of fullness or pain. During descent, there's increased pressure in the outside air. If the ears and sinuses cannot ventilate, negative pressure is created inside these cavities. Negative pressure creates a vacuum, which can "suck" mucous into the sinuses and middle ears, causing congestion, pain, and increased risk of an ear or sinus infection, especially if fellow airplane passengers are shedding respiratory viruses. An individual with middle ear pressure and congestion may also have diminished hearing and crackling sounds in their ears. Some experience vertigo (dizziness).

Keeping the ears and sinuses well ventilated with rapid changes in atmospheric pressure may take effort. Yawning and swallowing open the Eustachian tubes to let air flow freely. Sucking on a hard candy or chewing gum helps adults to frequently swallow. If the ears feel stuffy, "popping" one's ears requires gently exhaling, while pinching the nostrils closed and keeping the mouth shut. This can also ventilate stuffy sinuses. Forceful exhaling with the nostrils and mouth closed will create too much air pressure and could potentially

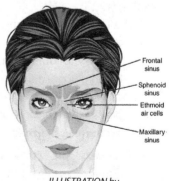

Frontal sinus
Sphenoid sinus
Ethmoid air cells
Maxillary sinus

ILLUSTRATION by Wikimedia Commons

rupture the eardrums, (**barotrauma**), so **popping one's ears** should be done with **slow, very gentle exhalation**. Young children who do not know how to "pop their ears" are especially susceptible to earaches with altitude changes. They should be encouraged to drink during ascent and descent so that swallowing will help them to ventilate their middle ears.

Being able to pop the ears or sinuses may not be possible if there's congestion due to respiratory infection, allergies, or other problems. Some, but not all people who are prone to ear and sinus problems, can prevent travel-related trouble by taking an over-the-counter oral decongestant such as pseudoephedrine, or an over-the-counter nasal spray containing phenylephrine or oxymetazoline. Acetaminophen, or an NSAID such as ibuprofen or naprosyn can ease pain. Warm compresses to the face or external ear may be soothing.

A rare but possible adverse reaction to rapid ascent is hemorrhage in the eye causing **diminished vision**. This usually resolves. Also very rarely, **acute anxiety** may be associated with rapid ascent to high altitude. In a group of more than 1,000 marine infantrymen exposed to altitude similar to Park City, seven servicemen who had no symptoms of AMS, developed acute, severe anxiety. Also rarely, rapid ascent to high altitude unmasks a **seizure disorder**, but people with well-controlled seizures are not usually at increased risk.

One more risk of high altitude exposure could be **carbon monoxide poisoning.** Cooking in tents or failing to ventilate RVs, boats, or snow shelters can readily cause carbon monoxide poisoning at any altitude, but at higher elevations, it's more rapidly fatal.

Avoiding Altitude Problems

Notice: Information provided in this book should not be substituted for evaluation and advice from a personal health care provider who is familiar with your health status.

In the following situations, people can usually tolerate high altitude with some extra precautions.

- People with **diabetes** may need to more closely monitor their blood glucose and adjust medications. The hypoxia of high altitude can trigger stress hormones that raise blood sugar. There's also a possibility that some **glucose-measuring devices may be less accurate** at high altitude and cold temperatures.

- Some people with **well-controlled asthma** may do better at high altitude, particularly if they have allergic asthma, since there's less dust and pollen. However, asthma sufferers should be prepared in case an attack occurs. Sometimes people who have breathing difficulty are mistakenly diagnosed with asthma instead of altitude intolerance.

- People who use CPAP machines for **sleep apnea** are at increased risk of altitude problems. If sleeping accommodations are planned to be above 5,250 feet (1,600 m), people with sleep apnea should consult their personal physician as to whether a special kind of CPAP machine or preventive medication is indicated.

- **High blood pressure** is generally not a risk factor for high altitude travel, but blood pressure tends to increase with ascent. In persons with unstable blood pressure, monitoring is advisable, as is travelling with a plan to alter medication if necessary.

- The combination of altitude and cold may increase the risk of heart attack in persons with **cardiac stents**, who should make extra effort to stay warm.

- **Migraine headache** sufferers are not more prone to AMS, but if they develop a migraine, they may mistake it for AMS, or vice-versa. If usual migraine treatment is ineffective, supplemental oxygen might help.

- Persons who have suffered **traumatic brain injuries,** or who suffer from extreme **obesity,** and **smokers** may be at increased risk for AMS. **Consider slow ascent.**

- Sleeping agents may relieve **insomnia** due to high altitude, but can also depress respiration. They should be used very cautiously if not completely avoided.

- **Alcohol depresses respiration** and **increases dehydration.** It is best to avoid alcohol until one is certain that high altitude is not going to adversely affect them.

Persons with pre-existing conditions noted on the next page might want to **avoid travel to altitudes above 6,560 feet (2,000 m)** unless there's a way to promptly descend to lower altitude, or access supplemental oxygen.

Healthy people who have never previously been to high altitude can reduce their chances of having a problem at altitude by taking the following precautions:

- Be **conditioned** enough to comfortably exercise at lower altitudes, before attempting strenuous activity at higher elevations.

- If possible, **ascend** to your destination **gradually.**

- **Become familiar with the symptoms of high altitude illness** and **have a plan** for descending to a lower altitude should you become symptomatic.

- Have your personal physician provide you with **precautionary prescriptions** for supplemental oxygen, acetazolamide or other measures needed for your circumstances.

Health Conditions That May Preclude Travel to High Altitude
- Unstable angina pectoris*
- Moderate to severe heart failure
- Cyanotic heart disease
- Other severe heart disease
- Prior to a coronary intervention
- Within three months of a heart attack, stroke or implantation of a cardioverter device
- Poorly controlled asthma
- Severe COPD (Emphysema)
- Cystic fibrosis
- Pulmonary arterial hypertension
- Sickle cell anemia
- Cirrhosis with portal hypertension
- High risk pregnancy**

*A graded exercise test at sea level may help to identify persons with angina pectoris who should not travel to high altitude.

** It's generally agreed that pregnant women with high blood pressure, preeclampsia, or poor fetal growth should not travel to high altitude, especially after the 20th week. Rapid changes in altitude might also increase the risk of premature labor due to changes in pressure against the amniotic sac. For women visitors with healthy pregnancies, slow ascent may be prudent.

The website of the International Society for Mountain Medicine at *www.ismmed.org* is a reliable resource for both health professionals and the public regarding the prevention and treatment of high altitude illness.

What About Chronic Exposure to High Altitude?

Little is known about the effects of living at a moderately high altitude like Park City. Much of the high altitude research that is currently emerging comes from higher Colorado. One difficulty of studying the effects of high altitude residence is that the people who migrate to higher elevations tend to be healthier than the general population. Also, older people tend to migrate to lower elevations, skewing statistics to a younger population. It's unknown how many older people might move downhill because they can no longer get a good night's sleep.

It is known that **babies born at higher elevations are small**. A large, 30-year study across the European continent revealed that for every 1,000 meters (3,281 feet) of elevation, babies weigh about 150 grams (5 oz) less than babies born at sea level. They also show lower oxygen levels. The long-term consequences of smaller birth weight and low oxygen are not yet known. However, there is data showing that babies born at very high altitudes, in the Andes and Himalayas, have bigger lung volumes and greater exercise capacity throughout their lives, than do people who live at high altitude, but who were born at lower elevations.

There's some increased risk of pregnancy complications such as hypertension and eclampsia at high altitude, but the risk of birth defects due to a virus like Zika is reduced because the mosquitoes that transmit the virus are rarely found above 2,000 feet (607 m).

High altitude residence also increases risks of **skin cancer, cataracts, dry eye syndrome**, and overgrowth of the surface of the eyeball, (**pterygium),** due to increased exposure to ultraviolet light. (Learn more about UV light in the chapter on sun, sight and skin.)

Also increased at high altitude are rates of **respiratory diseases, multiple sclerosis** and **suicide**. The incidence of **depression** is higher in Utah, Colorado, Wyoming, Idaho, Montana, Nevada, Arizona, and New Mexico, than in the other 42 states where people live at lower elevations. Researchers suspect that chronic exposure to low oxygen is associated with chemical changes in the brain that may lead to depression and suicide in some persons.

The effects of living at high altitude on **high blood pressure** are mixed. Some individuals show slower progression of hypertension while in others, blood pressure might rise. Reasons for this paradox are unknown. High altitude may put some people at risk for **high-altitude renal syndrome (HARS),** characterized by high blood pressure, an excess of red cells in the blood, and chemical changes in urine. It's diagnosed by laboratory tests and may respond to medication.

High altitude may increase the risk of **pulmonary hypertension,** a serious condition that taxes the heart. Symptoms include fatigue, shortness of breath for routine activities, decreased appetite, pain in the chest and abdomen, and a racing heart. Diagnosis may require echocardiogram and/or heart catheterization. Treatment includes moving to lower altitude, symptomatic care with medication, oxygen and sometimes, lung transplant.

Sleep disorders are consistently associated with high altitude living. Insomnia, nighttime awakenings, less restful sleep, and more sleep-associated breathing problems such as **apnea** are related to low oxygen. However, even at sea level, sleep quality and quantity declines with aging. People in their 80s tend to get little deep or consolidated sleep at night. Many "cat-nap" during the day to make up for the deficit.

There are also **benefits to high altitude living,** such as a **lower incidence of obesity**. Colorado, with an average altitude of 6,800 feet (2,073 m), is the only state in the U.S.A. with an obesity rate < 20%. Even volunteers placed in a simulated high altitude chamber for 40 days, and allowed to eat anything they wanted, still showed significant weight loss.

Data from Colorado also suggests that living at high altitude is associated with **lower death rates due to heart disease, stroke, diabetes,** and **cancers** of the lungs and colon. **Life expectancy may be longer.**

Finally, what little is known about the effects of high altitude living may apply more to a town like Breckenridge, Colorado at 9,600 feet (2,926 m) than to the more moderate altitude of Park City. Some researchers believe that **living at moderate elevations may confer more benefits than risks.** Much more research is needed.

High Altitude and Athletic Performance

Interest in the effects of high altitude on athletic performance skyrocketed in 1968, when the Summer Olympics were held in Mexico City at an altitude of 7,382 feet (2,250 m). Multiple world records were shattered for runners and jumpers at these games, and many of those records lasted decades until broken in competition in other high places like Colorado Springs.

It's now understood that performance at high **altitude will be better for** athletes who perform in **explosive sports** like sprints, broad jump, and triple jump. The reduced atmospheric pressure decreases resistance against the body surface; and if acclimated to thinner air, the athlete can jump farther and run faster for short distances. Organizations such as the International Association of Athletic Federations (IAAF) have ruled that athletic records set at elevations above 1,000 meters (3,281 ft) will go in the books with an attached "A" for altitude.

It's also now believed that **altitude works against endurance athletes**. For races longer than 800 meters (half-mile), the oxygen deficit catches up with the athlete and his/her time will be slower than at sea level. It was previously believed that athletic performance would improve if athletes trained at high altitude, but in many cases, the athletes didn't benefit because they couldn't train as hard at altitude as they could at sea level. **Training at levels above 8,000 feet (2,438 m) is generally not recommended.** This altitude level stimulates the release of stress hormones, which contribute to weight loss, muscle wasting, and decreased performance levels.

The current thinking for athletes is **"live high** and **train low."** Living at high altitude increases the number and proficiency of red blood cells to carry oxygen from lungs to muscles. High altitude living is sort of a natural method of blood doping (the outlawed practice of transfusing a stored quantity of one's own blood before a competition, or illegally using blood boosting drugs to increase red blood cell numbers). In addition to violating the ethics of competitive sport, unnatural methods of blood doping pose risks such as infection, blood clots, heart attacks and strokes.

Living at high altitude does more than boost red blood cell production. Acclimatization also increases the number of blood vessels to skeletal and heart muscle, the quantity of myoglobin protein in muscles, and the production of the enzymes that metabolize oxygen. These changes provide benefits not gained by illicit blood doping, Some of the benefits of high altitude depend on **proper nutrition.** Iron is especially important for red blood cell function. Meatless diets may cause iron deficiency, especially for menstruating females, who may require dietary supplements. Some athletes will also need increased calorie intake to offset the weight loss effects of high altitude.

How long acclimatization should take is debatable. One formula suggests that the number of days needed to fully enrich blood is the product of altitude in kilometers x 11.4. For Park City's 7,000-foot (2,134 m) elevation, that computes to 24.3 days. In reality, most visitors arrive and ascend rapidly without any difficulty, so this formula is more relevant to athletes trying to achieve peak performance than to visitors trying to enjoy some hiking.

Park City is considered an ideal training elevation for elite athletes and serves as the home of the US Ski and Snowboard teams. For the 2014 winter Olympic Games in Sochi, Russia, more than 60 Olympic competitors lived in Park City. Local training facilities for bobsled, luge, skeleton, ski jumping, Nordic and alpine skiing, and half-pipe aerials are the best in the country. Ice skating rinks in Park City and Salt Lake City make Park City the home of some renowned skaters who live high and train low.

Living or exercising in, or visitation to, a high altitude environment can have some profound effects on bodily function, health, and athletic performance. Knowing about altitude related risks and being able to recognize them should they occur, is the best way to manage altitude adjustment.

Sun, Sight, and Skin

The Sun is your friend, but like many friendships, you need some limits to exposure. Understanding the effects of solar radiation will help hikers make optimal choices in protection.

Waves of energy moving through space are referred to as **electromagnetic radiation**. The **visible light spectrum** includes the energy waveforms that human eyes can see as light and the colors of the rainbow, but most waveforms are invisible to humans, except for the specially equipped.

Electromagnetic Radiation and Sight

Several components of light are known to be harmful to the human eye, particularly visible blue light and invisible ultraviolet light. **Blue light** is emitted by computer, TV, phone and other electronic screens, and by **LEDs** (light emitting diodes) and **CFLs** (compact fluorescent lamps), in addition to being emitted by the Sun. The whiter artificial light appears, the more blue light it emits. **Ultraviolet (UV) light** has several different waveforms:

- **UVA** has the longest, slowest wavelengths and is least damaging, but penetrates glass.

- **UVB** has more energy that can **burn skin** and **eyes,** but is mostly blocked by glass.

- **UVC** has very intense energy and is very damaging to human tissue. Fortunately, **ozone** in Earth's atmosphere absorbs most of the UVC, which is why we must protect ozone.

    Acute intense UV light exposure from the Sun or artificial light can cause eyes to tear and burn. A welder whose goggles slip while using a torch that emits high levels of UV radiation could incur a **"flash burn".** In another scenario, someone who spends a day on snow or water without proper eye protection might experience a **"slow burn",** with symptoms appearing several hours after exposure. In severe cases, as with **"snow blindness"** (photokeratitis), the cornea is burned and vision is impaired. With proper treatment, eyes usually heal. First aid includes cool compresses and light avoidance. Prompt medical attention is advised for worsening vision or pain.

    Cumulative blue and **UV light exposure** contributes to the development of **cataracts, age-related macular degeneration (AMD)**, and cancers and noncancerous growths on the eye (pterygia and pingueculae).

    UV exposure is increased by being outdoors **at high altitude.** The thinner atmosphere of higher elevations absorbs less UV energy. For every 1,000 meters (3,281 ft) increase in elevation above sea level, there's a 10-12% increase in the level of UV radiation. Blue light is also more intense at higher altitudes. To have a lifetime of good vision, **sunglasses are recommended for all outdoor activity,** and should be worn at **all times of day,** even on cloudy days and especially at high altitude. They should also be worn in the car because side windows of many cars do not block UVA. Neither do many tinted windows. Front windshields should.

The U.S. Food and Drug Administration (FDA) requires that sunglasses block 99% of UVA, and be relatively shatterproof on impact. Other countries have broader standards, and many manufacturers offer lenses that block both UVA and UVB, up to wavelengths of 400 nanometers. Such glasses are usually labeled "**UV400**" or "100% UV protection." Optometrists can measure the UV protection level of your eyewear if you're curious.

Ideally, **sunglasses should be large enough to cover the eyes,** have **side shields** that block UV light coming in from the sides, and have **enough curvature to fit the face** and prevent UV light from coming in from the cheeks or forehead. **Hats with visors further protect the eyes**.

Polarized lenses improve vision for drivers, boaters, skiers, etc. by reducing glare, but **polarized lenses do not provide UV protection**. Look for sunglasses that provide UV protection, and polarization if desired. Although expensive sunglasses usually have better quality lenses, they provide no more UV protection than inexpensive sunglasses that meet basic consumer standards. If you consistently wear glasses that adapt to bright light by automatically darkening, you probably have optimal UV protection. Make sure **children** are wearing good sunglasses too. The younger the eye, the more susceptible it may be to UV damage.

Avoid very dark lenses, which cause the pupils to enlarge to let more light in, resulting in increased penetration of UV and blue light. Lens color actually has no effect on the level of UV protection. Even clear lenses can block blue and UV light. Clear blue blocker lenses are recommended for people who spend a lot of time looking at computer screens. There are also screen filters and apps that reduce blue light exposure, though the success of preventing old-age vision problems by use of these filters is not yet known. Yellow lenses may improve visual contrast in low light environments, like skiing on a cloudy day.

Finally, the best sunglasses won't protect you if you don't wear them. As much as **80% of the Sun's light comes through clouds**, even on very overcast days. Fresh snow can also reflect 80% of solar UV radiation. Being near, in, or on water can increase solar radiation by 25%. Sand adds about 15%. Just wearing a white t-shirt reflects some UV light into your face and eyes. Some level of solar radiation penetrates eyes during all hours of daylight.

Electromagnetic Radiation and Skin

Sunscreen products have been widely available since the 1950s but the chemicals in them keep changing. Nonetheless, evidence shows that consistent use of sunscreen helps to **retard photo aging of the skin**, and **prevent squamous cell carcinoma.** To date, it appears that dedicated sunscreen use may not significantly reduce the risks of other skin cancers such as **basal cell carcinoma** and **melanoma.** There are also concerns that sunscreen use contributes to **vitamin D deficiency,** a growing problem as people spend less time outside.

What sunscreens do best is **prevent sunburns.** However, they also give people a false sense of security about sun exposure. By facilitating tanning without burning, **sunscreens induce many people to overexpose themselves to UV radiation.** Ironically, with increasing sunscreen use, there are rising rates of skin cancer worldwide. Depleted ozone in Earth's atmosphere may be largely responsible, but it's more likely that decreased ozone along with increased sunscreen use are raising cancer rates, because people aren't doing more sensible things, like wearing protective clothing and seeking shade when the sun is strong.

Some important issues to consider:

Always Avoid Sunburn! A few bad sunburns make the risk of cancer skyrocket.

The **Sun is strongest between 10 am** and **4 pm.** Some weather forecasts include a **UV Index,** to predict how much UV radiation will get through hourly. The index goes from 0 at night to 12 when UV is strongest. Readings of 6 or higher mean that without protection, eye and skin damage is likely. Readings of 10 or higher mean damage is occurring.

How much protection you need depends to what extent your skin is sun sensitive. Skin type is determined by how much of the pigment melanin you have.

Fitzpatrick Scale of Skin Sun Sensitivity

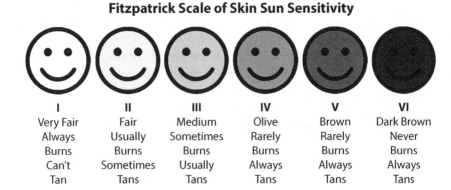

I	II	III	IV	V	VI
Very Fair	Fair	Medium	Olive	Brown	Dark Brown
Always Burns	Usually Burns	Sometimes Burns	Rarely Burns	Rarely Burns	Never Burns
Can't Tan	Sometimes Tans	Usually Tans	Always Tans	Always Tans	Always Tans

Melanin, found in skin, hair, eyes and other tissues, has the capacity to absorb solar UV energy. Apparently human skin colors evolved to allow just the right amount of UV light in. Human skin is darkest near the equator where UV radiation is strongest. Skin became paler as humans moved away from the equator where UV is weaker. The melanin of light-skinned people is less absorbent. It lets in more UV radiation in less time and provides little protection against burns and cancer. Having a lot of highly absorbent melanin as seen in dark skin, protects from burns and cancer, but makes it hard to get adequate amounts of vitamin D. People with darker skin may need increased sunlight exposure to avoid vitamin D deficiency.

It should be noted that regardless of skin type, even for those who never burn, **sun exposure** still **ages the skin,** causing it to **freckle, wrinkle** and **sag.** If you hike when solar radiation is strongest, your best protection is wearing UV resistant clothing, a wide brimmed hat, appropriate sunglasses, sunscreen on your face and hands, and a nice walk in shady woods. Gloves and facemasks are alternatives to sunscreen. If you hike in the early morning or evening, your risk of overexposure is reduced.

The **safety** and **effectiveness of** sunscreen ingredients are **unsettled** issues. In 2012, the U.S. Food and Drug Administration restricted the use of some potentially toxic ingredients, and banned use of marketing terms like "waterproof," "sunblock," "sweat proof," "instant protection," and "long lasting" since evidence to support such claims is inadequate.

The **SPF (Sun Protection Factor)** number on sunscreens provides mystifying math about UVB blockage as noted in the accompanying table. No product blocks 100% and SPFs higher than 45 do not provide better protection.

No product is stable enough to last more than a few hours. Manufacturers can only claim a waterproof factor of 40 or 80 minutes.

SPF (Sun Protection Factor) of Sunscreen Products		
SPF Rating	Protection Level	% UV Radiation Blocked
15	Fair	94
30	Good	97
45	Very Good	98

The **Environmental Working Group (EWG)** is a research nonprofit whose mission is "to empower people to live healthier lives in a healthier environment." They annually review numerous consumer products, and their sunscreen reports are extensive. In 2015, 80% of 1,700 sunscreen products were judged to be either potentially toxic or inferior for sun protection. Some popular products were assigned to the EWG "Hall of Shame."

Some Questionably Safe Sunscreen Ingredients These ingredients are **found in many cosmetics** in addition to sunscreens.		
Vitamin A and derivatives: retard skin aging but may induce growth of skin tumors in the presence of sunlight	*Hormone disruptors: associated with endometriosis in women and altered sperm production in males*	*Can cause allergic and photosensitivity reactions*
vitamin A	oxybenzone	avobenzones
retinyl palmitate	octinoxate	Octyocrylene
retinyl acetate	homosalate	benzophenone-3
retinyl linoleate	octyl methoxycinnamate	
retinol		

Sunscreens that use mineral filters titanium dioxide and especially **zinc oxide** are considered safest. These substances provide excellent UV protection but tend to leave a white film. The use of these minerals as sprays should be avoided. They are **toxic if inhaled**.

Increasing consumer awareness has been prompting manufacturers to start to offer sunscreen products that boast zinc and titanium oxide ingredients on their front label, including generics offered by some big chain pharmacy/retailers. **Read the label anyway**. Some of these products contain additional ingredients such as those mentioned above. You can see up-to-date results about specific products at *www.ewg.org*.

How sunscreen is applied impacts its effectiveness and safety. Spray sunscreens leave gaps more readily than hand applications. Don't forget temples and ears. Reapply if perspiring. Use a sunblock lip balm often. The EWG reviews these too.

Babies and young children are especially vulnerable to sunburn. **Infants younger than six months should be kept out of direct sunlight.** They have thinner skin and little melanin for protection. Older babies and toddlers should have hats and clothing that covers them as much as tolerable, and waterproof sunscreen with an SPF of at least 30 should be applied to exposed skin. The EWG specifically reviews the safety of sunscreens for babies. With appropriate protection, infants and children should get outdoors as often as possible.

Persons planning some fun in the Sun should avoid sunscreens in combination with anti-inflammatory agents such as ibuprofen, naprosyn, and many prescriptions. These drugs can reduce skin redness and pain so that a sunbather doesn't notice the burn. Redness is the warning signal that you are absorbing too much damaging radiation and need to get out of the Sun.

Certain medications can provoke a "photosensitive" or "phototoxic" reaction, causing skin to burn more readily than normal or cause a nasty rash. Check with your pharmacist or drug information websites to determine if your medication warrants extra UV precautions.

Sun-blocking hair products may or may not reduce sun damage to hair, but an appropriate hat is effective. A **hat with a tight weave** and **full brim of at least three inches (7.6 cm) width** also provides protection for the face, neck and ears.

UV protective clothing is another option for reducing sunlight overexposure. Most opaque clothing blocks some UV light, but a thin white cotton t-shirt lets about 20% of the Sun's rays through, more if wet. Synthetic fabrics like elastane (Lycra®) are best at block-

UPF (Ultraviolet Protection Factor) Ratings of Fabric and Clothing		
UPF Rating	Protection Level	% UV Blocked
15-24	Good	93.3-95.6
25-39	Very Good	96-97.4
40-50+	Excellent	97.5-98+

ing UV light. Nylon and polyester are second best. Some manufactures label their products with another confounding numeric system, the **UPF**.

There are also UPF dyes and washing agents to improve UV blocking power, though their effectiveness is uncertain. Washing fabrics improves UV blockage by causing some shrinkage, making the weave tighter. Wearing elasticized clothes that are too small reduces UPF, because the fabric becomes more porous if stretched out.

Unless you are headed for a river expedition or some other outing with limited escape from the Sun, UPF rated clothing is probably unnecessary. Tightly woven fabric that covers up most of you, and sunscreen for the rest of you, is all most hikers should need.

The Sun is the most effective and natural source of vitamin D. **If you need some UV light to boost your vitamin D level,** you can absorb beneficial rays with unprotected exposure of your legs between your socks and shorts.

Adults with **vitamin D deficiency** have increased risks for many diseases and premature death. The list grows as human sun exposure declines. Deficiency of vitamin D in infancy and childhood causes **rickets**, characterized by deformed bones and stunted growth. Apparently nature intended for infants to get their vitamin D from sunlight, since human breast milk, rich in other essential nutrients, lacks vitamin D. Recent research suggests that children who do not get adequate sun exposure in early life are also more likely to be nearsighted than children who play outdoors.

Some Diseases Associated with Vitamin D Deficiency

- Osteoporosis
- Bone fractures
- Fibromyalgia
- Breast cancer
- Prostate cancer
- Colon cancer
- Other cancers
- Diabetes
- Cardiovascular disease
- Obesity
- Sleep apnea
- Depression
- Multiple sclerosis
- Autoimmune disease
- Psoriasis
- Alzheimer's disease

Persons who limit their sun exposure should have their vitamin D levels checked in both summer and winter, and seek medical counsel regarding nutritional supplementation if increased sun exposure isn't possible. Excessive oral intake can lead to toxicity.

In conclusion, UV light is essential to human health. Everyone should be concerned about overexposure, but not to the extent of risking underexposure. Being out in sunlight for 15-30 minutes two to four times a week is a reasonable goal, along with maintaining a healthy diet rich in fruits and vegetables. Orange vegetables such as carrots and squash provide carotenoids, which help combat UV stress. Eating healthy fats, as opposed to processed vegetable oils, also improves defenses against oxidative stress caused by UV radiation. Avoiding smoking further enhances the body's ability to combat the aging effects of UV light exposure.

So, keeping the Sun as a friend, while limiting exposure and protecting our skin and eyes, can be another benefit of hiking.

Footwear and Foot Issues

Research about foot function and footwear is limited in both quantity and quality. Conclusions are often based on studies of athletes or soldiers whose level of fitness and foot use differs from that of most people. Hikers in particular are a diverse group, and one person's footwear heaven may be another's hell.

Meanwhile, the shoe industry keeps trying to come up with new ideas to promote sales. Some inventions become global trends but others become bargain basement boobie-traps. Popularity of a shoe speaks nothing of its performance. Millions think the world of the venerable flip-flop, but foot doctors think it's one of the unhealthiest shoe designs ever created. It requires unnatural leg lifting to overcome the "flop," stressing the ankle and knee joints. It promotes sprains of the ankle and foot.

Low Top Trail Running Shoes vs. High Top Hiking Boots		
Feature	**Low Top Trail Runners**	**High Top Hikers**
Break-in time	None to little break in needed	Can take many miles and days
Comfort	Light, well ventilated, many options for good fit	Heavy, stiff, can get sweaty. Superior warmth for winter
Weight	1-1½ lbs. (0.5-0.7 kg) Lighter shoes reduce fatigue and improve agility and ability to move quickly	2-3 lbs. (0.9-1.4 kg) Heavier weight can impair efficiency, agility, and speed
Ankle support	Lace-up ankle braces inside the shoes can support weak ankles	Better for weak ankles, especially lace-up boots
Durability	Need more frequent replacement	Last longer
Safety	Easier to stub a toe. A thorn or cactus spine can penetrate. More apt to collect pebbles and debris	More protective of feet and ankles against poison ivy, brambles, debris, snakes, etc.
Tread	Inadequate on wet surfaces	Better for most surfaces, especially snow
Water resistance	Not resistant. Dry out quickly if wet	Resistant but if submerged they take a long time to dry
Maintenance	Some are washable or brush clean	Brush plus leather care
Adaptability	Limited. Less adaptable to orthotics	Can add **crampons** for snow. Better able to support a heavy hiker or hiker carrying > 25 extra pounds (11 kg)
Cost	Many price points	Usually more expensive

The favorite hiking shoe design of the recent past is no longer considered ideal. Heavy, high top, drab hiking boots have given way to low top, lightweight, colorful trail runners. Ankle support designed into the high top shoes of yesteryear, is now thought to restrict a hiker's ability to adjust foot position in response to the varying surfaces of a natural trail. Restricted ankle motion may therefore increase, instead of reduce, the risk of turning an ankle. It's also theorized that high top shoes may inhibit the ankle joint's ability to generate power, increasing stress on foot and knee joints and increasing fatigue. Studies of athletes and soldiers in high top and low top footwear have not shown benefits of the high top in preventing injury or improving performance. In 1982, the US Army switched from physical training in boots to running shoes, and a 2015 study showed no difference in the injury rate after getting rid of the boots.

Actually, options go beyond just these two choices. In recent years, retailers offered at least **seven shoe types** for hikers. Choice should be guided by what kind of hiking you plan to do and in which type of shoe can you get the best fit. Before you check out the hiking shoe options in the next table, know that there are no hikes in this guidebook that require rock climbing or scrambling over rough terrain. Unless conditions are slippery, most people should be able to safely hike most of these trails wearing basic athletic shoes that are in good condition.

Fit is as important if not more important than most any other shoe feature. Hiking in shoes that slip on your heels or pinch your toes should be avoided at all cost. Most hikers do best in a hiking shoe **one-half to one size up** from their regular shoe size, since hiking feet tend to get puffy in hot weather. In colder weather, there's room for a heavier sock. Always test new shoes on short walks before hitting the trail.

Make sure your hiking shoes are not past their prime. Loss of tread impedes safety, and loss of cushioning can cause foot problems. Shoes **wear out** about every 500-600 miles (805-966 km), depending on your weight, gait, walking surface, degree of perspiration, etc. Hiking in worn out shoes is asking for trouble.

Wear good quality **socks** that are well cushioned. Holes or thin spots in your socks show where there is excessive pressure, usually at the heel or the ball of the foot. Wearing socks with holes causes even more pressure on these areas. If you hike a lot, choose synthetic socks with wicking materials to help keep the feet dry in hot weather, or for sweaty feet. Clean and **moisturize** your feet before you put on clean socks. Optimal skin hydration helps avoid friction. Cotton socks are not recommended as they absorb perspiration and increase friction. Longer socks provide more ankle protection than low-cut socks. Take

Choose Hiking Shoes Based On the Kind of Hiking You Plan to Do			
Shoe Type	Shoe Features	Pros	Cons
Barefoot or Minimalist	Thin soled, like gloves with toe compartments. A relatively new trend; Injury rate under study.	Greater feel of the trail. Better exercise for foot muscles.	Not protective against sharp rocks, thorns, or stubbing toes.
Basic athletic	Your typical low top sneakers.	Fine for occasional hikers on moderate trails.	Less sturdy or durable as types noted below.
Trail runners	Like basic athletic but extra padding, stiffer soles, more tread and ankle support.	Lightweight. Lots of options for getting a good fit.	Not protective enough on slick or rough terrain.
Approach	Hybrid with features of a rock climbing shoe and a trail runner. Stiff toes prevent twisting.	Ultra-light. Extra grippy for edging along rocks. Lace to toes for custom fit.	Not grippy enough on slick or wet terrain.
Light hikers	A little beefier than trail runners. Still low cut.	More tread for technical terrain but still lightweight.	Fewer options than trail runners. Heavier.
Mid-weight boots	High top favorite prior to the rise of trail runners.	More durable. Better tread. Good for most terrain. Waterproof.	Heavier. Need a break-in period.
Mountain -eering boots	Heavy, stiff boots for prolonged backpacking or rugged terrain.	More durable and supportive for long hikes and heavy loads.	Heaviest. Need a lot of break-in. Not for casual hikers.
Hiking sandals	Open toe shoes of any type are NOT RECOMMENDED for Park City trails.		

along an extra pair of socks for a potentially wet hike. In winter, avoid allowing your feet to become **very cold.** Tendons are more vulnerable to inflammation when feet are very cold for a few hours. Wool or wool/synthetic socks are warmest.

Footwear accessories are another whole industry. Even the **insoles** that line your hiking shoes can be a consumer conundrum. Also called **foot beds,** insoles can do all kinds of things for your feet and your shoes. Proprietary insoles, heel cushions, metatarsal pads, etc., like those of Dr. Scholls®, Footbalance®, Superfeet®, etc., can improve the comfort, fit and performance of shoes.

However, these products don't take into account that the left and right feet often differ, and what helps the left foot may cause a problem on the right.

Custom insoles are often called **orthotics**. They can support the arch, relieve pressure points, improve foot alignment and solve other foot problems. Orthotics are typically prescribed by a foot specialist such as a podiatrist, though technology now enables any shoe seller who can afford the machinery to create "customized" foot beds. Meanwhile, researchers have installed sensors in insoles to learn more about foot activity and stress during various activities and in different kinds of footwear. Look for these "**smart insoles**" to become increasingly available for athletes seeking performance improvement, and for foot pain sufferers seeking relief. Heated foot beds are available for seriously cold feet. Antimicrobial compounds have been incorporated into some shoe insoles to help people who are prone to stinky feet.

Gaiters can keep shoes and feet dry in wet conditions, and clean on dusty trails. Gaiters are waterproof leggings that strap over low-top trail shoes. They weigh much less than waterproof boots. Short ankle gaiters can also help keep dirt and debris out of mesh top shoes and are easier to clean than shoes. Some hiking shoes come with gaiter connector systems. Numerous companies sell gaiters online.

A good **brush** is an important accessory for shoe maintenance. Getting mud, dirt, and other undesirable stuff off of the tops and out of the soles of your hiking shoes preserves their function and helps them last longer. Some shoes are washable. Leather cleaners and conditioners protect leather boots from drying out and can help preserve water resistance.

By Johnny.m76 - Own work,
CC BY-SA 3.0,
https://commons.wikimedia.org/w/
index.php?curid=31668150

Crampons are contraptions that strap onto shoes to provide traction on snow or ice. There are several types ranging from lightweight chains to metal plates with multiple sharp spikes. Step-in crampons require certain kinds of boots, while strap-on crampons can adapt to most shoe types.

Cord (round) **shoelaces** are less likely to attract burdocks and thorns than flat laces, but the knot may be slippery. Double or triple-knot them to avoid a lot of shoe tying. Flat shoelaces provide a better knot but soak up water and snag on plants. D-ring laces, consisting of a thin cord with a locking mechanism, can be un-repairable if they break along a hike. Rawhide laces can be stiff and break more easily than other laces. There are also waterproof laces. The type of shoelaces you choose may have more to do with the threading system on your shoes than the material of the laces. Know the size of the eyelets and the length of the old laces before selecting new ones. Extra shoelaces can serve hikers in many ways.

If shoelaces loosen when threaded through hooks at the top of a hiking boot, lace "over and down" the hooks instead of lacing "under and up". The laces will then loop around the hook and hold better.

Foot problems are a tremendous burden for people, whether or not they hike. Preventing foot problems is well worth some extra effort. It is also important to recognize problems when they first arise and treat them appropriately before they become more serious or debilitating.

One of the most avoidable problems for the novice or occasional hiker is the **Over-Did-It-Syndrome (ODIS)**. (That's a term made up by the author, so you won't find it in a medical dictionary.) Taking a longer hike than one is accustomed to, or in extreme temperatures, or on extreme terrain, or in the wrong footwear, can result in screaming feet. Avoid ODIS by knowing the nature of a hike before accepting an invitation.

If, on some occasion, a long hot hike in not-so-comfy shoes leaves you with screaming feet, one possible remedy for people with normal circulation is a "cold plunge" or what physical therapists call an ice bath. Just before getting off of your poor, tired feet for a long rest, get a pot or pan big enough for a foot, and dump some ice cubes and enough water in to allow foot submersion. Then, if you can tolerate it, "white-knuckle" it for a few minutes of foot submersion on each side and expect a quick recovery.

A happy pair of feet is the most essential ingredient to the enjoyment of hiking. If you want your tootsies to last a lifetime, take excellent care of those cold little, hardworking, and essential body parts.

Common Foot Problems and What to Do About Them		
Problem	About	What to Do
Athlete's foot (tinea pedis) or stinky feet	Shoes can harbor fungus, yeast or bacteria. Use manufacturer's washing instructions. If they can't be washed, remove laces and insoles, pull out the tongues and leave them in sunlight for a few days. Decontaminate shoes to successfully treat feet.	OTC products may be effective. Lotions containing peppermint and eucalyptus applied to clean feet may inhibit fungus. Seek medical consultation if stinky or itchy, cracked skin persists.
Capsulitis	Inflammation around a joint, often in the ball of the foot. Very painful. May be due to shoes that are too flexible or too stiff for your feet.	Stop hiking. Rest and ice for 5-10 minutes 3-4x a day. If no progress in a few days, seek help. Orthotics or new shoes may be needed.
DOMS = Delayed Onset Muscle Soreness	Muscles asked to perform in an unaccustomed way do it, but are achy and tender the next day. DOMs is a common form of ODIS (Over Did It Syndrome) that most everyone has experienced, but it hasn't been well studied.	NSAIDs, massage, icing, hot tub jets, stretching, and other remedies may help. Avoid hiking until better. Learn to listen to your body and condition and pace yourself.
Planter Fasciitis	Pain in the heel and sole of the foot. Pain is worst with first few steps. May be related to footwear but can suddenly appear or disappear for uncertain reasons. Hiking may not be possible.	Most cases resolve in 6-12 months, though it can be chronic or recurrent. Some people get relief from night splints, orthotics, massage, stretching, or platelet rich plasma (PRP) injections.
Sprains of the **ankle** or **foot**	Stretching or tearing of tendons and ligaments around a joint. An ankle may twist if ground gives way. Any joint can be sprained but a weight-bearing joint sprain on a hike is an issue. Hobbling on uneven terrain risks more injury.	Get off your feet. Pull the front of the foot up towards the knee to try to relax stretched ankle structures. Rest awhile. An ace wrap may help. Call for rescue if it's too painful to bear weight.
Stress fracture or **"march fracture"**	Incomplete bone fracture due to overuse. Most often the 5th metatarsal (pinky toe side of the foot). Can affect the tibia (shin bone) or patella (kneecap). Persistent pain is the primary symptom. Diagnosis is by x-ray.	Get off a painful foot as soon as possible. Consult with a podiatrist (foot specialist) or orthopedist. Some fractures require surgery to insure proper healing.
Tendonitis or **shin splints**	Tendons attach muscles to bone. Shin splints affect the fronts of the legs. The Achilles tendon in the ankle and the quadriceps tendon are other tendons that can become painful due to inflammation or degeneration. ODIS, hiking hills, running on hard surfaces, or over or under foot pronation can all be causes.	Forget hiking until better. Rest and ice the tender areas for 5-10 minutes 3-4x a day. NSAIDs like naprosyn or ibuprofen may help. Seek medical consultation if persistent. A footwear change or orthotics may be needed if recurrent.

Gear and Gadgets

One of the great things about Park City hiking is that you're never very far away from town or emergency assistance. Of the 45 included routes in this guidebook, none takes you more than 10 miles (16 km) from the heart of town. For hikes this short, there are just three essential things to take along: an adequate supply of **water, UV protection**, and for lone hikers, **identification**. Include information as to who to notify in an emergency and any pertinent medical history. Perhaps a **cell phone** should also be considered essential. Most all of Park City and local trails have cell phone service.

An **adequate supply of water** is critical to replace fluid lost through respiration and perspiration. With every exhalation, moisture in the breath depletes the body's reserves. Sweat may immediately evaporate and go unnoticed. The more strenuous the hike, the more water is lost. For high altitude visitors, there's additional water loss through increased urination.

Considering that most people don't drink enough water anyway, quadrupling of usual water intake may be prudent for those partaking in strenuous exercise at elevations to which they are unaccustomed. Many people won't feel enough thirst to motivate them to increase their water intake spontaneously, so it's advisable to make a conscious effort to drink more water, especially if it's hot. As noted in the altitude chapter, increased water intake may alleviate symptoms of acute mountain sickness. Both **dehydration** and **acute mountain sickness** can cause **headache, fatigue, nausea**, and a feeling of **weakness**. Hiking while feeling fatigued and weak increases the risk of injury.

Potable water sources convenient to the hikes in this guidebook are scarce. Do not count on natural water sources for hydration. Mountain streams contain high levels of heavy metals, possibly bacteria and other contaminants. Carry enough water for yourself, and the kids and dogs if they're unable to carry their own. Also, don't underestimate winter water needs. Respiratory water loss can be significant when exercising in cold, dry air.

To avoid dehydration, an adult should consume **2 cups (0.5 L) per hour of hiking**, more for very hot temperatures or vigorous hikes. Kids need 1-2 cups (0.25-0.5 L) per hour. Drinking water before setting out on a hike and taking sips along the way is the best way to stay ahead of dehydration. Water weighs about 2 pounds per quart (0.9kg/L), so starting out well hydrated takes some weight off your back.

Several types of **water-carrying systems**, including systems for kids and dogs are available. Backpack bladders with easily accessed mouthpiece tubing allow hikers to drink without stopping. Water bottles are heavier and bulkier than bladders, but better at maintaining cold. A hiker may be better-balanced carrying two bottles of water, one on each side of a pack, than a single large container that sways. Water bladders such as the CamelBak® are harder to clean and less durable than bottles. **Water containers should not be made of soft plastic.** Environmental heat causes harmful chemicals in plastic to leach into your beverage. The plastic that bottled water is sold in is the kind you should avoid.

For the sake of your sight and skin, please see the Sun chapter in this guidebook for important information about **UV protection** at high altitude.

In addition to water, identification, and UV protection, these gear options are recommended to help hikers be prepared for whatever might happen along the trail.

1. Unless you know the way, the very complicated Park City trail system demands that you bring this guidebook or some other **map** and a **compass**, to reduce the risk of getting lost. (Smart phones have compasses). Learn how to use them.

2. A fully charged mobile **phone**. An emergency charger is also a good idea.

3. A **mirror** and **whistle** for signaling (should the phone not work and you need help).

4. **Toilet paper** and sealable plastic bags to take it with you. (See **Responsible Hiking** for important information about using nature as a bathroom.)

5. A **first aid kit** that contains basics such as, (and in order of estimated importance):

    i)   Diphenhydramine to counteract an allergic reaction. If a person feels faint or shows rapid swelling or is wheezing after a bee sting, immediately give diphenhydramine, and lie the person down with legs elevated. Rescue is needed if symptoms worsen.

HOW TO DOSE DIPHENHYDRAMINE			
WEIGHT in POUNDS (Kg)	**DOSE ONE OF THESES FORMS OF DIPHENHYDRAMINE EVERY 4-6 HOURS**		
Under 20 lb., (9 kg), or 1 year: **DO NOT GIVE** *unless directed by a doctor*	**Liquid 12.5 mg/tsp (5 ml)**	**Chewable 12.5 mg Tablets**	**25 mg Tablets or Capsule**
20-24 (9-11 kg)	¾ tsp. (3.75ml)	NO	NO
25-37 (11-17 kg)	1 tsp. (5 ml)	1	½
38-49 (17-22 kg)	1½ tsp. (7.5 ml)	1½	½
50-99 (23-45 kg)	2 tsp. (10 ml)	2	1
100+ (45+ kg)	4 tsp. (20 ml)	4	2

ii)   Antiseptic wipes, bandages, and butterfly closure strips to clean and cover wounds. Thoroughly clean wounds before using any kind of skin glue. Gauze pads and a roll of medical tape, plus scissors, are more versatile than proprietary bandages. Antibiotic ointment is less important than good cleansing.

iii) Artificial tears can wash a foreign body or burning sunscreen out of an eye. The semi-sterile fluid can also be used to cleanse a wound.

iv)   Moleskin to apply to hot spots before blisters develop.

v)   Ace wraps or bandanas or even extra shoelaces to fashion a splint out of branches.

vi)   Tweezers and/or a multi-tool knife with scissors, tweezers, etc.

vii) Safety pins can turn a shirt into a sling and provide other options.

viii) A waterproof lighter to sterilize a pin to pop a blister. A lighter can serve other purposes, but making a campfire in Park City's drought stricken forests should NEVER be one of them.

i)   Antacid tablets for indigestion, and loperamide tablets in case of adult diarrhea. Consult with your personal physician about treating such problems in kids. An anti-itch remedy like calamine lotion or 1% hydrocortisone cream may also be useful.

ii)   Instant cold pack and acetaminophen for pain.

6. A **rain poncho** and/or a solar blanket and/or extra clothing.

7. A **flashlight.**

8. **Food** should include something sweet, like fruit, which can stave off low blood sugar (hypoglycemia), and something salty such as nuts, which can offset salt loss due to perspiration. Nutrition bars are an easy emergency snack.

9. Extra **UV protection.** Please see the chapter on sun, sight and skin.

10. A **pack** to carry it all in. A hiker should be able to fit all of the above (except water), into a small pack. Packs shouldn't unbalance a hiker by weighing one side down, as would be the case with a shoulder or handheld bag. Keep hands free for balance or trekking poles. An enormous variety of packs and water bottle carriers are available. The best way to choose one is to try it on, and see what size water bottles it accommodates. Some waist/fanny packs are so wide that water bottles collide with elbows. Some water bottle pockets are too shallow to support a decent-sized container. Some backpacks are too long, or have shoulder straps that are placed too narrowly or widely and might impinge nerves in the neck or shoulder. People who are extra large or extra small are more likely to wind up with an ill-fitting pack if they don't do an in-person try-on. Adventurous hikers should consider a pack made of waterproof material.

Hikers who have the luxury of planning their hikes according to an ideal weather forecast, and who know their route, can risk excursions with minimal provisions. Hikers whose plans coincide with less favorable weather or who are in unfamiliar territory should be well prepared for all contingencies. Retailers sell many types of pre-stocked hiker packs and first-aid kits, neatly encased. There are some excellent, compact first-aid kits available on-line for as little as $12.00. Solar blankets can cost less than $5.00 and serve many purposes. A well-prepared hiker can grab their ready-for-anything hiking pack in a second and limit prep time to fresh water and snacks.

Trekking poles, a.k.a. walking sticks, are a gear option to be considered. There are significant pros and cons to their use and some controversy about their ability to reduce wear on tear on the lower extremities. While using poles is a matter of personal preference, they can serve valuable functions. They're most helpful for providing stability on challenging terrain. While I personally like to hike with free hands, I will find a branch I can use as a walking stick if I find myself on loose rock or slick downhill ground. A pole or poles may be helpful for someone whose balance is suboptimal. Poles can also help probe for rocks, roots and other hazards hiding under fallen leaves.

Walking with poles (**Nordic walking**) increases calorie expenditure by increasing the number of muscles engaged in action. It's a better workout than just walking, but consider that with greater energy expenditure, one might fatigue sooner. Paradoxically, some pole users contend that poling boosts their stamina, perhaps because they use their poles very efficiently. Pole use may stress upper extremity joints. Some argue that poling is an unnatural activity that taxes shoulders and wrists. Others argue that engaging the hands with poles prevents hand swelling often seen in hot weather, by improving upper extremity circulation.

Using either one or two poles, a hiker should swing the pole forward with the hand opposite to the forward stepping foot. A poling technique on tricky terrain is to swing both poles forward simultaneously and then take two steps. Using one pole allows switching off hands to avoid fatigue.

For hikers who like poles, here's a synthesis of advice from some published experts: Though pole height is a matter of preference, having the elbow bent at 90 degrees while holding the pole with its tip on the floor is considered the optimal position. Telescoping poles that can be shortened for uphill hiking, and lengthened for the downhill, help maintain the optimal elbow position. However, they are heavier than fixed length poles, which may suffice for hiking level terrain. Telescopic poles can be collapsed and stuffed in a backpack.

Aluminum trekking pole **shafts** are lightweight. Some carbon fiber and composite materials are lighter, stiffer and better at shock absorption, but may not be as durable as aluminum. Spring-loaded poles absorb shock well but are heavier.

Cork is considered the ideal **grip** material. It's resistant to moisture, protects from vibration and temperature extremes, and conforms to the shape of the hand. Some people prefer the softness of foam, but it absorbs perspiration and needs frequent replacement. Rubber may be comfortable in winter, but not for a sweaty hand. Plastic handles should be avoided. **Grip extensions** give a hiker the option to choke up on the poles as opposed to shortening them. **Wrist straps are no longer recommended**. Hold your poles or store them in your pack, but don't drag them. Being attached to wrist straps increases the risk of thumb, hand, wrist, and shoulder injuries if a hiker falls.

Carbide **tips** may work best for hiking rocks. Metal tips work well but can break. Rubber tips grip best on the road. Baskets are good on snow or sand, but will snare if there's vegetation. Rubber tips that go over metal or carbide tips makes travelling with poles safer.

Many trekking poles are outfitted with a camera adaptation to serve as a monopod.

Hiking **clothing**, beyond shoes, socks and hats, needn't be anything special, so long as it doesn't restrict your mobility and is appropriate for UV protection and anticipated weather. Park City hikes can be quite chilly early on summer mornings, but the temperature rises quickly. On hot afternoons, there can be a rapid temperature drop when the sun disappears behind the mountains. Even on the most beautiful of summer days, a sudden squall of wind, rain, hail or even snow, can pop up unexpectedly, especially at higher elevations.

The best way to be prepared for weather changes is to dress in layers. My favorites are a waterproof, hooded, nylon windbreaker with mesh lining, weighing 8.5 oz, (240 g), and a puffy down vest, 5.5 oz, (160 g). Each can be folded up into a wallet-sized package and stuffed in a pack. I often start out in autumn in four layers. The windbreaker comes off first, then the vest, then the long sleeved turtleneck, and I'm down to a t-shirt. Long pants with bottoms that zipper on and off to become shorts are another convenient option. A **hat with a tight weave** and **full brim** of at least **3 inches (7.6 cm) width** provides UV protection for the face, neck and ears. A waterproof, wide brimmed hat and/or a thin plastic poncho are handy accessories on days with possibility of precipitation. On chilly days, gloves and a scarf serve well and are easily carried.

Some of the hikes in this book are at altitudes 2,000-3,000 feet (600-900 m) higher than the town of Park City. Anticipate a temperature drop of 3° F (1.8° C) for every thousand foot (305 m) gain in elevation (**adiabatic lapse rate**). That means if the Old Town temp is 45° F, (7.2°C), then it's likely 36°F (2.2°C) on Jupiter Peak. However during **winter inversions**, daytime temperatures may be higher on the top of the mountains than in the canyons below.

Wicking fabrics incorporated into today's athletic clothing do a good job of keeping us dry and comfortable in hot weather, but they are easily snagged by trailside vegetation. Until a better fabric comes along, you could carry a snag-resistant over-shirt in your pack and put it on over your "snaggable" top if trail vegetation gets gnarly.

Please see the chapters on footwear and UV protection for important information about shoes, socks, sunglasses and sunscreen.

For the hiking **family with a member who does not walk**, there are a variety of child and adult strollers designed for use on unpaved terrain. Some of the basic features to look for in an **all-terrain stroller** include large inflated wheels that can easily deal with obstacles and uneven terrain. A typical all-terrain stroller has one wheel in front and two in the rear. A good suspension system helps keep the rider from bouncing around. A multi-point harness also helps prevents bouncing and sliding out of the seat. Reliable brakes are critical for dealing with hills. Make sure there's a locking mechanism that will keep the stroller from rolling on an incline. Also desirable is storage space to pack water and gear. Make sure the stroller won't tip if there are heavy items in the storage bin. Features such as these along with lightweight construction can make all-terrain strollers quite pricey.

If you only intend to walk on paved terrain, you may be able to get good service from a less costly stroller that does not have all of these features. Options may be most plentiful on the Internet, but shopping for a stroller in person better enables you to make sure that the chair fits the rider and the pusher. A 25-pound (11.3 kg) stroller with a 30-pound (13.6) kg) rider can be challenging to push uphill.

Child carrying packs are discussed in the chapter on hiking with children.

As for **gadgets**, there's an overwhelming array of possibilities. Spotting scopes, night vision goggles, smart phone apps that identify flowers, trees, butterflies, etc., and all kinds of hiker emergency kits are available. One outdoor store boasted over 30 types of GPS systems people might use for outdoor navigation.

The beauty of Park City's trail system is that you can just go take a hike without any gadgets. Good footwear, UV protection, water, identification, this guidebook, and a pack to carry it in may be all you need. The hikes in this book are not long enough for hikers to need water purification systems, tents, and all the other gear available for backpacking. For interested persons, there are many excellent resources available regarding an astounding assortment of gear options for day hikes, backpackers and campers.

Useful Resources

Notice: URLs for websites seem to frequently change.

Bus Info
Free Park City Transit System
go.parkcity.org/InfoPoint/ or
parkcity.org/departments/transit-bus
435-615-5301

General Info
Park City Chamber of Commerce and Visitor Information Centers
visitparkcity.com
Park City Museum, 528 Main Street 435-649-7457
and Visitor Center @ Kimball Junction,1794 Olympic Parkway 435-658-9616

National Ability Center Sports and Recreation
Discovernac.org
1000 Ability Way (Quinn's Junction) 435-649-3991

Trails and Open Space Info
Mountain Trails Foundation
Mountaintrails.org
435-649-9619

Winter Trail Information
www.parkcity.org/departments/trails-open-space/winter-trails

Swaner Ecocenter
Swanerecocenter.org
1258 Center Drive, 435-649-1767

Summit Land Conservancy
wesaveland.org
435-649-9884

Park City Hospital
900 Round Valley Drive (NW of the intersection of US-40 and SR-248)
435-658-7000

News and Local Info
kpcw radio station FM 91.7 and on-line
kpcw.org
435-649-9004

The *Park Record* newspaper
Parkrecord.com
435-649-9014

pctv1 television station
Various channels and on-line
parkcity.tv
435-649-0045

Avalanche Information
Utahavalanchecenter.org
Recorded avalanche info: 888-999-4019

Local and Nearby Hiking Clubs
meetup.com/wasatchhiking
parkcitynewcomers.org/events/hiking
wasatchmountainclub.org
www.meetup.com/wasatchhiking/
eventbrite.com

National Hiking/Walking Organizations
americanhiking.org
www.ava.org
hikinglady.com/get-outside/organizations/
sierraclub.org organizes outings in which volunteers can partake in trail
development and maintenance.

Index of Trails and the #s of the Hikes in Which You'll Find Them

Acknowledgements

I am eternally grateful to the leaders and citizens of my adopted home of Park City who've made this town the hiker friendly place it has come to be. The support of my husband, Kenneth Hurwitz MD, in learning the trail system, the editorial assistance of my family members, Nancy Costo and Basu Ghosh, and input from Amy Schapiro were especially helpful to this book's development. And most valuable and critical to the successful completion of this project, was the thoughtful and generous expert assistance provided by Katie Mullaly, who served as cartographer, interior designer, and publishing and marketing mentor.

All uncredited photos and illustrations were taken or created by the author.

About the Author

Beverly Hurwitz, MD was born in Brooklyn, New York in 1948. She started visiting Park City in 1973 and has been a full-time resident since 1990. Prior to attending medical school in 1977, Dr. Hurwitz spent nine years teaching public school health and physical education. Her medical career includes training in physical medicine, neurology, pediatrics, and acupuncture, and she spent decades attending to patients with acute and chronic injuries. Since retiring from clinical practice, she has served as a medical expert and case analyst for administrative law judges in the Federal and Utah State court systems. She and her husband (and dachshunds) have been hiking around Park City for decades. She is also the author of *A Walker's Guide to Park City* and two novels: *Nobody Else's Business* and *Is the Cat Lady Crazy?*

Made in the USA
Coppell, TX
29 June 2022

79411441R00115